you&your
Audi TT

you & your

Audi TT

Ian Shaw

Buying, enjoying, maintaining, modifying

First published in December 2004

A catalogue record for this book is available from the British Library

ISBN 1 84425 102 0

Library of Congress catalog card no. 2004 112 996

Published by Haynes Publishing, Sparkford, Yeovil, Somerset, BA22 7JJ, UK

Tel: 01963 442030 Fax: 01963 440001
Int. tel: +44 1963 442030 Int. fax: +44 1963 440001
E-mail: sales@haynes.co.uk
Website: www.haynes.co.uk

Haynes North America, Inc.,
861 Lawrence Drive, Newbury Park,
California 91320, USA

Pagebuild by Glad Stockdale
Printed and bound in England by J. H. Haynes & Co. Ltd, Sparkford

Jurisdictions which have strict emission control laws may consider any modifications to a vehicle to be an infringement of those laws. You are advised to check with the appropriate body or authority whether your proposed modification complies fully with the law. The author and publishers accept no liability in this regard.

While every effort is taken to ensure the accuracy of the information given in this book, no liability can be accepted by the author or publishers for any loss, damage or injury caused by errors in, or omissions from, the information given.

Contents

Acknowledgements

My thanks are due to everyone involved in the production of this book, notably the following companies and individuals who supplied information, illustrations, guidance and inspiration.

The staff of the Audi UK Press and PR Department, namely Jon Zammett, David Ingram, Kate Dixon, Beverley Holloway, Loiuse Vukomanovic, Martyn Pass and especially Robin Davies, for his continual assistance.

All the staff of Audi Tradition in Ingolstadt, particularly Dr Martin Kukowski, co-ordinator of the Audi Archive, for finding the excellent pictures of the car's technology and development, and especially Lothar Franz, not only for his great assistance, but for affording me the opportunity of touring the 'secret' workshops adjacent to Audi Tradition's offices, and for generally making my 'Day in Ingolstadt' a memorable experience.

Jurgen Lewandowski, David Staretz and Herbert Volker, the authors of *The TT Story* produced by Delius Klasing, a documentary publication on Audi's design of the TT, which pointed me in the right direction on numerous occasions. Thanks also to the staff and instructors of The Audi Driving Experience.

I am grateful to Tim Wright and all the staff at LAT for their excellent photographs of the rally and race quattros, Simon Fox at Haymarket Publishing for the *What Car?* images of the TT on roadtest, EMAP Automotive for supplying the images of the modified TT, Simon Pelly at Rage Products for the component pictures, and Colab for supplying Audi UK archive images.

Thanks are due to Paul Harris of *Audi Driver* magazine, which is a constant source of excellent information. Finally, thanks to Andrew King for his tireless assistance with the detail photography of the Audi UK-supplied cars, and 'first draft' proof-reader, Brenda Shaw.

Ian Shaw
Dronfield,
November 2004

Introduction

The Audi TT has been idolised for its design flair, for its accessible performance, and for its sheer image. The Audi TT Coupé quattro and Roadster quattro provide traditional sports car values of style, performance and driving pleasure. This is coupled to a degree of practicality for touring and the legendary roadholding of the quattro four-wheel-drive system, something unique amongst sports coupés in the TT's category.

Unlike most sports cars, the Audi TT does not polarise, it unites. It brings together Audi's four-wheel-drive benefits for those who subscribe to the quattro heritage, and its revolution of motorsport and road car thinking in the 1980s, with radical styling for owners who choose the car for its design. These values are allied with Audi's superb level of engineering integrity and driver involvement.

Although always intended for production, the Audi TT is generally considered to have started life as a concept car that made it to the road with few changes. This is indeed a rare occurrence for a concept car and illustrates the TT's production-readiness from the very early stages, simply another example of Audi's lateral thinking on sports car design, and one further feature which sets the TT apart.

It is an illustration of the TT's clean design that so little has been changed since its inception. Like the original Ur quattro, Audi's TT is set for true classic status and will surely rank alongside the Porsche 911 for its combination of clean design and technical achievement.

Although utilising components that are shared with many models within the VW and Audi family, the TT has grown in unison with Audi's gradual move to a more upmarket image. Like its fellow German marques, Audi has forged its reputation for fine engineering, but has managed, in the TT, to marry this with a character which would more normally be the preserve of Italian sports coupés, few of which could hope to match the TT's level of engineering quality.

No wonder then, that the Audi TT is an icon.

For some, the Audi TT is about style, for others it is about driving. This 3.2-litre V6 example demonstrates both. (*What Car?***)**

Chapter One

The quattro –
a revolution

The Audi TT Coupé has something no other sports car has. A small badge, almost going unnoticed, tells of its unique underpinnings and its evolution from one of the most significant cars in the history of the automobile. The badge is inscribed, quattro. This one word makes the TT unique; it describes not only a revolutionary ancestor, but to many Audi enthusiasts it is a culture

Opposite: The TT turns heads in town but simply begs for the open road. (Audi Press)

Below: This little badge separates the TT from all other cars in its class. (Spectrum Media)

and a sense of belonging. It is quite simply the fulcrum on which Audi's entire fortunes turned.

During the 1970s, Audi was a maker of solid and dependable, if rather uninspiring family and executive cars. Its standing was in decline and the management craved a new direction for the marque. Engineering and technical abilities were at Audi's core and its development of the five-cylinder petrol engine in 1976 and use of turbocharging in the Audi 200 Turbo of 1979 were to hint at its next big step.

In the days before electronic traction control systems, Audi's engineers realised that their increasingly powerful and heavy cars were reaching the limits of

The revolution started here. A 1980 quattro in the Audi Museum, Ingolstadt. (Audi Tradition)

traction that front-wheel drive could deliver. Like most European revolutions throughout history, the one at Audi was a family affair. In 1978, Audi began production of the Volkswagen Iltis at its factory in Ingolstadt, Germany – a former VW site. This was a four-wheel-drive military vehicle in the same mould as the Jeep and Land Rover, for the West German Army. Audi's engineers immediately saw the potential to increase the traction in a performance car by utilising the four-wheel-drive components of the Iltis. Since the vehicle used a 1.7-litre (104cu in) engine from the Audi 80 and VW Passat, the layout would lend itself quite easily to that of contemporary Audi cars. An Audi 80 was thus equipped with a modified Iltis 4x4 system and the A1 – effectively a quattro prototype – was born.

Audi knew that the success and advantages of such a radical car would have to be proved to the buying public and that international rallying would be its logical showcase. In 1980, Audi entered four VW Iltis vehicles in the gruelling Paris–Dakar Rally, some of which were powered by Audi 200 Turbo engines, to test the reliability of the quattro drivetrain. All four finished the 10,000 mile (16,000km) event, and moreover, an Iltis won.

Although cross-country vehicles such as the Jeep and Land Rover had used four-wheel drive for decades, when Audi was developing the quattro system only one

DID YOU KNOW?

Audi's longitudinal engine layout was considered outdated for front-wheel-drive cars, but was ideal for the requirements of a 4x4 transmission.

high-performance road car had been made with four-wheel drive previously. Jensen, the small British luxury car maker had unveiled the Jensen FF (which stood for Ferguson Formula – its four-wheel-drive system) in 1966, this being based on the Interceptor 2+2 GT car. When production ceased in 1971, less than 400 of the Chrysler V8-powered cars had been built, so Audi knew the quattro would stand or fall on its level of public awareness.

In March 1980, Audi launched the quattro at the Geneva Motor Show. Although the company's intention was to offer a full range of four-wheel-drive road cars, it only expected to build 400 examples of the turbocharged five-cylinder coupé. This was the number required for homologation into rallying, but history recorded that it needed to build a good many more than that!

The quattro name would indeed spread across the whole Audi range in time, but for now, the focus is on the original quattro and its rallying career.

All the world's a stage

Audi's motorsport department signed 'Flying Finn' Hannu Mikkola to the team in 1980 to develop the quattro for rallying. Although it won the first event in which it was entered, the Janner Rally in Austria, a round of the European Championship, it was in the World Rally Championship which Audi had to succeed. For motorsport fans it was the Monte Carlo Rally of 1981 when the world changed. Mikkola set the fastest time on 8 of the 32 special stages before crashing out, but notice had been served.

On the Swedish Rally, the only event in the calendar with a guarantee of snow-covered roads, the quattro of Mikkola romped home in first place. Audi did not enter four of the 12 rounds in the 1981 championship, but still took Mikkola to third place in the drivers' table after a win in the RAC Rally of Great Britain, a third place in the 1000 Lakes Rally in Finland and a fourth place in Italy on the San Remo Rally. The 1981 San Remo was significant for another reason. Michèle Mouton and Fabrizia Pons became the first all-female crew to win a World Championship Rally in their quattro, and Michèle – with more quattro victories in

'Flying Finn' Hannu Mikkola, was the highly experienced driver brought in to develop the quattro rally car. (LAT)

subsequent years – is still the only woman driver ever to have won a rally in the World Championship series.

For Audi, 1981 proved a tough development year; its victory on the Swedish Rally could be seen as purely an expectation – a four-wheel-drive car on snow – and several crashes had proved that the massively quick car could be difficult to tame.

In 1982 however, Audi stamped its mark firmly on the rallying scene and the quattro was forever woven into rallying folklore, just as surely as the Mini Cooper, Ford Escort RS and Lancia Stratos.

Not only did Audi take the Manufacturers' Championship but won seven of the 12 rounds and gave

Left: Serving notice: the quattro on the 1981 Monte Carlo Rally. (LAT)

Above: Speed and glamour: Michèle Mouton, to date the only woman to win at World Rally Championship level. (LAT)

Right: Stig Blomqvist, World Rally Champion in 1984, with Audi taking the manufacturers' title too. (LAT)

Michèle Mouton another accolade. She took second place in the drivers' table beating male team-mates Mikkola and Blomqvist into third and fourth slots.

In 1983, the quattro carried Hannu Mikkola to the Drivers' title, with Blomqvist and Mouton fourth and fifth respectively while the Manufacturers' title eluded Audi by just two points, from Lancia. However, this was not enough for Audi and it was in 1984 that the real goal was achieved. The quattro did the double, delivering the Manufacturers' Championship for Audi and the Drivers' Championship for Stig Blomqvist with team-mate Hannu Mikkola taking the second place in the table that year.

However, for the 1983 season the full scope of the regulations governing the type of car that could be entered in international rallies had been changed. The

FIA, the governing body of the sport, had created a monster, which once released, would take rallying to new heights of excitement and public profile, but would ultimately come within a whisker of bringing about the demise of the entire sport. The monster's name was Group B.

Power corrupts

Essentially, Group B did one thing: it cut the number of cars that needed to be built to allow a model into rallying, from 400 units to just 200. This paved the way for the rally supercars, specials that bore no more than a passing resemblance to road cars and which boasted mid-engined configurations, four-wheel drive, and over 400 horsepower.

Above: A car for the conditions: the quattro dominated where traction was the key. This is Mikkola on the Monte Carlo Rally. (LAT)

Below: The quattro was equally at home in the dry dust of Portugal. This is Röhrl in 1984. (LAT)

This is the rare Sport quattro, road versions of which were built to homologate the Group B rally car. (Audi UK)

It was Audi's answer to these cars, its doctrine of maintaining as strong a link as possible with its road-going cars, and the desire to retain its motorsport exploits as a road-car marketing tool, which took them down the path of the sports supercar. It would eventually lead to the creation of a true road-going sports car – the TT.

Other manufacturers created Group B cars which had spaceframe chassis designs, like a grand prix car, mid-mounted engines and four-wheel drive. Many had only one component in common with the road car upon which they were supposedly based, and that was the windscreen!

Audi knew it had to do two things in the light of the Group B supercars: increase the power and cut the weight and size of the quattro. Its solution was simple, but hardly subtle. Audi literally cut 12in (305mm) from the wheelbase of the quattro and left the front and rear sections the same. It then doubled the number of valves in the head of the five-cylinder engine and wound up the turbo's boost. The resulting Sport quattro – christened 'short-quattro' by many – was a weird-looking device, but with 450bhp on tap, was nothing if not effective.

The road-going Sport quattro was unveiled at the Frankfurt Motor Show in the autumn of 1983 and its 20-valve engine could muster some 306bhp, giving it a performance to match the true supercars of the day, from the likes of Porsche. This engine was to feature more widely in the road cars from 1989, so Audi's motorsport developments were truly improving the breed.

The Sport quattro was difficult to drive, its front-engined layout and heavy frontal weight bias making for tricky handling in the chopped wheelbase chassis. However, Audi was determined to stick to its doctrine that the rally cars must share as much with the road cars as possible – certainly in the basic shape, driveline layout and engine type.

DID YOU KNOW?

Less than 200 of the 214 Sport quattros built were ever offered for sale to the public. Audi used many, and Walter Röhrl owned one of the first to be produced.

Above: The Sport quattro on the 1984 Acropolis Rally in the hands of Walter Röhrl who made no secret of his dislike for the car. (LAT)

Right: Walter Röhrl, who tamed the Sport quattro. (LAT)

The car was gradually developed and the long wheelbase original was run alongside it on most events, with the team's reward being a win for Blomqvist on the Ivory Coast Rally. This was Round 11 of the 1984 season and the first one the Sport quattro had finished. Ironically, in the face of the opposition from supposedly more advanced mid-engined competitors, the conventional quattro had taken wins in six previous rounds that year with quattros taking first, second and third places in three of the rounds, in Monte Carlo, Sweden and Argentina. All these results contributed to that Audi double: the 1984 Manufacturers' Championship and the Drivers' Championship for Blomqvist, with Mikkola second in the table for good measure. In the face of more specialist opposition all of which had followed Audi's lead with four-wheel drive, the quattro had taken both crowns, with only a minor contribution from the Sport quattro. The development of the original recipe had taken the most honours.

This picture of the Sport quattro in plan view shows the car's short length-to-width ratio. (LAT)

The 1985 season was to be Audi's last full championship year, although nobody knew this at the time and Audi was on top form as the season began. The Sport quattro had been developed further and its often unruly handling tamed to some extent, although the power of its 20-valve engine now exceeded 500bhp. The evolution version of the car grew wings, which despite impressions you might have had to the contrary on seeing it fly through the air on the infamous crests of the 1000 Lakes Rally – were intended to give it better grip on the track, as the engine in this Sport quattro S1 was now rumoured to be producing the best part of 550bhp. In years to come, Audi would use the engine in the American IMSA GTO racing series with 720bhp, still from just five cylinders and 2.2 litres (134cu in).

In rallying however, the 1985 season concluded with two second places for Audi. Second in the Manufacturers' Championship and a second place for Stig Blom-

qvist in the Drivers' Championship. Audi only won one World Championship rally that year, the awesome Sport quattro S1 crushing all before it on the San Remo in Italy, in the hands of Walter Röhrl although Mikkola took a conventional quattro to victory on the Hong Kong–Beijing event.

Nobody could foresee the dark days ahead, as the 1986 season began in Monte Carlo, in January. Rising young star Henri Toivonen won, in his Lancia Delta S4, with Sport quattro S1s taking third and fourth places. In Sweden, Audi campaigned the new 90 quattro, before heading for Portugal and Round 3 in March. This event was the beginning of the end for Group B. The Southern European rounds had become increasingly notorious for poor spectator control while Audi and Ford had both complained strongly in their press conferences in

Above: Frequent flyer: the Sport S1 quattro on the 1000 Lakes Rally.

Below: Blomqvist at home on the snow in the Sport quattro. (Both LAT)

Portugal was a disaster waiting to happen. Here Blomqvist shows the finer points of car control and manages to avoid the crowds. But it was too close for comfort – for the driver anyway! The spectators evidently felt quite safe. (Both LAT)

Above: Dark days for rallying: Group B cars were to end. (LAT)

Below: The awesome Sport S1 quattro in a final fling. (LAT)

The more specialised Group S was to replace Group B, but died with it. Audi's prototype was banished to the Audi Museum, Ingolstadt. (Audi Tradition)

previous seasons about the situation in Portugal. Drivers had to rocket down narrow tracks lined deep with spectators literally inches from the cars, many standing in the path of the car until the very last moment.

In Portugal that year, the teams' worst fears were realised. Local driver Joaquim Santos in a privately entered Ford RS200 crested a rise at very high speed to find the road completely blocked by a group of spectators. Trying to avoid them, the Ford went into the crowds beside the road and four people were killed and 30 injured. All the top drivers immediately withdrew from the event, refusing to drive out of the next time control.

Eight weeks later, Henri Toivonen's Lancia plunged off the road in Corsica when comfortably leading the event. Crashing into the trees the car was immediately engulfed in a horrific fireball. Toivonen and co-driver Sergio Cresto, perished.

The FIA announced that Group B was to be no more. The 1987 season would be for Group A cars, much more closely related to road-going machines, all of which within a year, would be four-wheel drive and turbocharged with a whole raft of road cars being produced to allow them to be rallied. Audi, having changed the face of rallying forever, withdrew from the international stage, and now set about doing the same thing to circuit racing.

To new challenges

In 1988, Audi entered three cars in the TransAm NASCAR series, not with the quattro which had dominated in European rallies, but with a huge luxury-limo of a car, the 200 quattro. It had the older 10-valve engine, although it was tuned to 510bhp, a six-speed gearbox and, naturally, permanent four-wheel drive. It won its second race and with consistent results backed by Germans Hans Stuck and rally-ace Walter Röhrl, the American driver Hurley Haywood took the Drivers' Championship title and Audi the Manufacturers' crown. Not bad for rookies!

The following year, Audi turned its attentions to the North American IMSA GTO Championship, with the smaller Audi 90 quattro. The drivers were Haywood and Stuck, but despite consistent results the drivers' and manufacturers' titles eluded Audi, although the decision not to enter the Daytona and Sebring events at the start

Audi took the quattro stateside, achieving great IMSA success with the 90 quattro. (Audi UK)

of the season must have been a significant factor. As it was, Audi took the second place in the Manufacturers' Championship with Stuck and Haywood taking third and fourth in the driver's rankings.

Audi also won the famous Pikes Peak Hillclimb in Colorado for three years in succession. This event is a timed run up a 12.4-mile (19.4km) gravel road with 156 corners leading to its 14,100ft (4,300m) summit. It was Mouton's Sport quattro in 1985 which added yet another accolade to her portfolio as the world's leading female driver. American legend Bobby Unser Snr drove another Sport quattro in 1986 with the (now 600bhp) Sport quattro S1 of Walter Röhrl getting to the top in just 10min 47.8sec, in 1987, beating a gaggle of other Group B refugees from Ford and Peugeot.

Back in Europe, Audi saw another opportunity to show the quattro system's prowess. In Touring Car races in Germany it beat the likes of BMW, Mercedes-Benz and Opel, with the unlikely and rather bulky V8

DID YOU KNOW?

VW also built a 4x4 rally car prototype on its Scirocco coupé. It used two engines, the second one in place of the rear seat, to give four-wheel drive.

quattro. Hans Stuck used it to convincingly clinch the driver's title. In the UK in 1996 Frank Biela took the British Touring Car title in an A4 quattro some 100 points clear of his closest rival and this with 209lb (95kg) of ballast as demanded by the sport's ruling body to try to compensate for the advantage of four-wheel drive.

In 1997, the British Touring Car organisers announced a certain way to penalise the all-conquering Audis. For the following season, four-wheel-drive cars would be banned.

Through 1996 the A4 quattro took seven Touring Car series championships around the world. Audi had proved that not only was the quattro superior on snow and gravel, but on tarmac too, and not just in the rain.

What a pedigree to have in any sports car, especially one that had just been shown in its first form at the 1995 Tokyo Motor Show; the Audi TT was ready to reap the rewards of all those competition miles.

Road cars, the real winners
It is difficult to think of either the competition quattros, or the road cars in isolation. They are more

Above: Audi beat its German rivals with the huge V8 quattro. (LAT)

Below: In the UK, the A4 quattro took BTCC honours. (LAT)

akin to two sides of the same coin, and even at the original quattro's launch the situation was clear. The road car would be developed to allow homologation of the rally car, the rally car would feed its development in the rigours of competition, back into the road car.

The quattro was unveiled at the Geneva Motor Show in March 1980. It had a 2.1-litre (128cu in) five-cylinder engine with 10 valves and a turbocharger. It produced 200bhp and torque of 210lb ft. Its performance stood at 138mph (222kph) maximum speed and an acceleration of 0–62mph (0–100kph) in 7.1 seconds.

An impressive enough specification for any four-seater coupé of the day, but of course the big news was the permanent four-wheel-drive transmission. The five-speed gearbox's torque was fed through three differentials, the centre and rear of which could be locked out for increased grip on mud or snow, to share the tractive effort through all four wheels. The traction benefits were obvious and had been used for decades in off-road vehicles but the world was about to be introduced to a new dimension in grip and roadholding for a powerful performance car.

Superlatives flowed from every press report on the quattro. Here was a car which could access all its power all of the time, yet was as docile and predictable as a front-wheel-drive car with half the power. It could bring cornering speeds to the moderately skilled driver in a four/five seat coupé, which had been the preserve of experts in mid-engined sports cars.

Sure, it wasn't perfect, the boot was rather small; it was a nose-heavy car so entering a corner too fast could produce considerable understeer and with so much grip, if the driver did exceed its capabilities, the quattro could be quite a handful to get back into line.

Icon for a generation: the Ur quattro. (Audi UK)

Generally speaking, in 1980, the driver's nerve would give out before the car's grip.

In the UK, the car was available from March 1981 but only in left-hand-drive form. At around 88 per cent of the price of a Porsche 911 SC it was not cheap, and the Porsche had a higher top speed. Only 160 quattros were imported to the UK in 1981, but the cult status was assured and demand began to rise. Right-hand-drive versions arrived from October 1982 and the quattro was firmly established in what was to become one of its most significant markets. The car was steadily improved, ABS became standard from 1984 and in 1987 the quattro transmission saw its first big change since launch. The centre differential unit was now a Torsen (torque sensing) device built by the American Gleason company. This unit gave better handling by virtue of allowing anything from a 50:50 front-to-rear torque split, to 25:75 in either direction. It removed the need for a centre differential lock to be operated by the driver and made the car easier to drive in mixed snow and wet-road conditions. The rear differential lock was retained and the engine grew to 2.2 litres (134cu in). The Torsen differential was first used as a limited slip device between the rear wheels of grand prix cars

before Audi used it in the quattro. It is also used in the huge US Army Hummer.

The next big step, in 1990, was the widespread use of the 20-valve engine, first seen in the shortened Sport quattro 'homologation special' of 1984. In the full-size quattro this engine produced 220bhp and some 228lb ft of torque. This latter figure, with revised gear ratios and that Torsen differential giving even better grip, meant that 0–62mph (0–100kph) acceleration took just six seconds and the top speed was 142mph (228kph).

The rare Sport Quattro, of which just 214 were made, all in left-hand drive, did much to raise the quattro's image still further. The modified 20-valve engine had 306bhp, a maximum speed of over 150mph and acceleration from rest to 62mph (100kph) in just five seconds. Its supercar status was equally well assured by a price tag to match Porsche and Ferrari and was, by far, the most refined of the Group B homologation road cars. It had a proper interior with 2+2 seating in leather while most Group B road cars were rather hastily built and some were not true road cars at all, but privateer rally cars.

The Ur (pronounced 'oor' and coming from the German for original) quattro, as it was now referred to, continued in 20-valve form until 1992. By then Audi had

spread the quattro net further with the 80 quattro in 1982 and coupé quattro, which ironically, did not appear until 1984 boasting four-wheel drive. Despite its bodyshell being shared with the Ur quattro, the coupé had been only front-wheel drive since 1980.

The 90 quattro and 100 quattro had joined the fray in 1984 and 1985 respectively and the luxurious 200 quattro was seen from 1985 onwards. All these models lasted until 1996 when Audi's entire model range went to its 'A' designation and the A4 quattro arrived. The A6 and A8 quattros with their V6 and V8 engines had appeared in 1994, but the marvellous five-cylinder warble of the turbo quattro was not to be silenced just yet.

The S2 Coupé, known universally as simply the S2 quattro, appeared in 1990 and was meant to be the successor to the Ur Quattro, but the two were sold side by side for over two years. The S2, and the rare RS2 Avant, both built by Porsche for Audi, utilised the same 20-valve engine, but with a more aerodynamic shape, were faster than the Ur quattro, and cheaper too, as the latter was still hand-built. The S2 had virtually no competition history, enthusiasts never took it to their hearts, sales were slow, and it had a lifespan of less than half that of its illustrious forebear. An era of motoring history had ended.

Above: The comparison between the shorter Sport quattro on the left and Ur quattro on the right is clear here. The A4 acts as a benchmark. (Audi UK)

Below: The classic lines of the Ur quattro continued until 1992 . . . (Audi Tradition)

... although the S2 Coupé, intended to be a replacement, which appeared in 1990, had a shorter life. (Audi UK)

The new breed

Audi had achieved its goal from those distant days in 1980: it had spread its quattro four-wheel-drive technology through every car in the range – there were executive cars and estates, and with its constant rise in European markets many quattro models were powered by diesel.

However, Audi had not forgotten its sporting roots, or the people who had made the quattro breed a success, and once again they would have a turbocharged quattro.

The A6 and A8 models were a different type of quattro as they were made to compete with BMW and Mercedes-Benz in the executive sector and it was left to the A4 quattro to try to recreate those heady days. With a 193bhp V6 engine, a Torsen centre differential and the advent of EDL (electronic differential lock) – in which the ABS system applies the brake to a spinning wheel to feed the power to those which have grip – the A4 quattro had broadly the real-world performance of the Ur quattro in 10-valve form. It had none of its negative characteristics of turbocharger lag or on-limit handling tantrums. However, despite its worldwide touring car racing success, it lacked that certain something. Enter the S4 quattro which was true to the quattro's roots. Audi's engineers took the A4 quattro, fitted it with a twin-turbo V6 of 265bhp and some 295lb ft of torque

and lowered its suspension by 20mm (0.8in). The result was a serious performance saloon. However, the A4 was a serious-sized saloon too and Audi looked in yet another direction for its quattro technology to be used. It was time to think smaller.

The route to TT

The Audi A3 had arrived in 1996. In the big scheme of things it was not earth-shattering news and for many it was merely a further indication of Audi and VW sharing not only components, but entire cars. The A3 was, in effect, an Audi version of the VW Golf (Rabbit in the USA). However it had a number of interesting features. It utilised the already proven 1.8-litre (110cu in) four-cylinder, five-valves-per-cylinder, turbo engine and even mated this to a quattro four-wheel-drive system. Although this took the quattro name, the four-wheel drive mechanicals were considerably changed from any quattro that had gone before. The reason for this was another change from traditional Audi design thinking: the engine was mounted transversely, as in the Golf. This gave obvious benefits in the packaging of a smaller car yet allowed Audi to retain four-wheel drive for high-performance requirements. The S3 quattro did just this with a 225bhp version of the four-cylinder, five-valves-per-cylinder engine, which Audi even referred to as the 20-valve engine! So, we had come full circle and in 1999, enthusiasts could buy a compact, 20-valve turbo quattro, with room for five people, a reasonable luggage bay and performance to embarrass bigger high-performance cars, just as enthusiasts almost 20 years before, had been able to.

Conceptual thinking

Audi, in common with most manufacturers likes to showcase its new technologies with concept cars. It had launched the Ur quattro without warning, but to those with a keen eye, the road to the TT was signposted with clues. One, although poles apart from the TT's execution, was the quattro Spyder concept car. Unveiled to an open-mouthed press core at the 1991 Frankfurt Motor Show it had Audi's original competition doctrine for the quattro running through it, that it should be as close to the road-going cars the public could buy, as was possible. To that end it had a 2.8-litre (171cu in) V6 from the A4 mounted transversely amidships, driving a quattro transmission by using a conventional differential on the end of the gearbox, whose half shafts were replaced by what were now the front and rear propshafts. Add the Torsen internals and the quattro Spyder was tantalisingly close to being a production car. Its aluminium body gave it a weight of just 1,100kg (2,424lb) with the V6 engine and, to justify the Spyder name, its central glass roof panel was removable, and stowed over the engine cover, while the vertical rear window was retractable. Finished in vivid 'Fidji orange', it was the star of the Frankfurt Motor Show. Press and public acclaim knew no bounds and the car embarked on an American tour, resprayed in a more subtle metallic green. This led people to believe a second car had been built, but there was only ever the one. It is now back in its orange colour, in Audi's museum.

Audi received 3,000 provisional orders for the quattro Spyder, and in late 1992 a full-scale non-running model of a revised Spyder with slightly longer wheelbase and doors was built. Audi even began talks with a low-volume builder to produce the quattro Spyder, but the envisaged costs led the Audi board of management to axe the project. It would simply have been too costly to build it at Audi's quality levels.

Just as the Avus supercar concept had wowed the visitors to Tokyo in 1991, as described in Chapter Two, it was the Japanese show in 1995 that Audi chose to show its latest sports car thinking. Unlike the Avus quattro this would not be an undrivable show car, and unlike the quattro Spyder it would not use so many unique parts that tooling for production would be out of reach. It had its engine in the front, mounted transversely while the floor pan was that of the A3. This was as near production-ready as any concept could be and was already shown in coupé and convertible forms: the TT and TTS were here.

Fruitless in orange: what a pity the gorgeous quattro Spyder was axed. It now resides in the Audi Museum, Ingolstadt. (Audi Tradition)

Chapter Two

TT – a new designer label

It is popular to comment that all modern cars look alike, and that the designs of the classic era of the 1960s and '70s have been forgotten. Of course, this is an overgeneralisation of the true picture. Family cars are designed by size and packaging requirements, and do indeed all conform to the same basic parameters. Front-wheel drive with a small four-cylinder engine offers easy packaging of the powertrain and a low rear floor height with a lifting rear tailgate gives ease of loading, and the cabin needs seating for five. Add some dimensional limits and the compact family car takes shape. In fact, they all take the same shape.

Sports cars however, need not conform to the same strict requirements. They might have four seats in the case of modern-day grand tourers, they may take the form of compact two seaters, or even a single seat is a more recent trend towards minimal comfort 'track' cars for those looking for an antidote to the family five-door.

There is a further factor. If the car is merely a product designed to do a job, then it should be purely functional, but the car is so much more than this. It embodies feel and emotion, masculinity or femininity, weight or subtlety, strength and protection. So, the car designer is often described not only as a designer, but also as a stylist. Nowhere else in the field of consumer items, does style play as big a part in a design as it does in that of the car. Its functionality is hidden, the engineering elements which make it go, turn and stop are hidden, only their tactile feedback is of concern, only the dynamic result important. Like architecture, the strength and form can be combined, and those who combine it to best effect with regard to style will be feted. This then, is the car designer's challenge.

Opposite: The glamorous TT quickly became the car to be seen in. (Audi Press)

The stunning Avus concept car showed Audi's design flair. (Audi Tradition)

Strength and form are no strangers to Audi. Throughout its history the company has been driven by its engineering innovation and integrity. Its lateral thinking brought the five-cylinder engine design into the petrol arena, its widespread development of turbocharging brought power rewards without fuel penalty, and on that note, today's diesel engine technologies have shown the direction to take at every new restriction brought about by legislation. Audi did not lack in design, but up until the 1980s, it did lack in style.

It is with some irony then, that the most visually striking car Audi had ever produced came about, not by a shallow styling exercise, or by a desire to merely create an attention-grabbing design on an existing vehicle, but by their intention to demonstrate the design

DID YOU KNOW?

The name TT is in homage to the great races of the same name. From 1911, riders on machines from NSU – one of the four companies later to form Audi – competed in the event with great success.

The Avus was not just one car; a number of styles were considered. (Audi Tradition)

qualities of its new body material: aluminium. The first production Audi to use it would be the A8 luxury saloon, and the car to give it impact was the incredible Avus.

Flexing the design muscles

The Audi Avus was intended to show the visual impact of the aluminium bodywork by being polished to mirror effect, it was also to recreate the halcyon days of the marque, long before the quattro had rewritten the motorsport rule book. Named after the famous 20km (12.4-mile) long circuit near Berlin, which opened in 1920, it was a latter day version of the famous silver arrow racing cars of the era, whose giant V16 engines had allowed them to dominate European racing in the 1930s. Its closest inspiration had come from the 1938 Auto Union Type D, a mid-engined V12 monster.

The Avus too would be mid-engined and, initially, thoughts turned to recreating the V16 by bolting together two Audi V8s, but the resulting engine would have proved simply too long. It was here that the W12 engine concept was born. Technically interesting, the W12 had three banks of cylinders, with four cylinders in each bank: think of it as a 120° V8 with an in-line four-cylinder engine dropped down into the Vee. It is compact, since the offset required for the connecting rods to pass each other and reach the crankshaft is minimal. It is, in effect, no longer than an in-line five-cylinder unit, but the W12 engine in the Avus concept car was actually a very carefully carved and painted block of wood.

So how does this showstopper of a car relate to the TT? In simple terms, where the quattro was a turning point for Audi in its image of engineering innovation, the Avus marked the turning point for Audi's innovation in style. There was a quattro four-wheel-drive system

with Torsen centre and rear differentials with an electronic front differential – itself the first hint at Audi's current EDL (electronic differential lock), used in the quattro system. It had four wheel steering too, and a pressure monitoring system for the tall but narrow 225/60 R 20 Goodyear tyres. These were specially produced to hint at the tyres of the 1930s cars. The car even had a usable luggage space. Audi also built one with a V8 engine to show it as a working car, since although the W12 engine was fine in concept, it could never have been produced in time for the Avus to be unveiled at the Tokyo Motor Show in 1991. Its W12 engine was a fake; the rest of the car worked however.

Two years later and Audi built a fully operational W12 engine and showed it, once more, at Tokyo. Speculation grew that the Avus would be built; Audi would not only take on Ferrari and Porsche but also potentially crush them. The rumour machine went into overdrive, would Audi build perhaps ten of these cars at astronomical cost, for multi-millionaire car collectors, would Audi race such a car at Le Mans? All came to nothing. The financial implications of building the Avus were too high, even to contemplate its production. The W12 engine did make it to full production though, but in a different form. The production engine has four banks of three cylinders, in effect, it is two narrow-angle V6 engines. This makes it even more compact than the original W12 concept with its three banks of four layout.

Not building the Avus only drove more people to think that the concept shown earlier in the year at Frankfurt, the quattro Spyder, might be built, but of course, that proved not to be. The reason for leaving both cars as museum pieces, was the same in both cases; the cost of building a unique sports car. Audi needed to combine the strong muscular lines of the Avus with the more practical and perhaps prettier lines of the quattro Spyder. It also had to do all of this on an existing mechanical layout if it were ever to build a sports car in sufficient numbers, and at an affordable price.

Current core, future face

This then was the design brief for the Audi TT, or as it was known in the beginning, the A3C – for A3 Coupé. Based on the A3 platform, with its engine mounted transversely in the front, gave the designers their fundamental parameters, the rest however, was up to them.

After the quattro Spyder's failure, particularly in the light of the enthusiastic response it had received, this ability for any future coupé to be built on an existing platform was paramount. Peter Schreyer, then Head of Audi Design, later said of the early days of the TT's design: 'We knew perfectly well that we couldn't build a car capable of enhancing the company image if we economised at every possible opportunity, but we wanted to keep in touch with reality so that the cost controllers didn't destroy our dreams once again.'

At the same time, Development Engineer Dr Ulrich Hackenberg and his colleague, Ralf-Gerhard Wilner had presented an idea to the then Technical Director, and subsequent President of the Board, Dr Franz-Josef Paefgen. The idea was for a shortened A3 platform, not

Cold light of day: the Avus would have been ultra-expensive to build. (Audi Tradition)

The quattro Spyder was a near-production-ready mid-engined car . . . but despite public adoration, it was axed. (Both Audi Tradition)

How fitting that the Avus and quattro Spyder are side by side in the Audi Museum. (Audi Tradition)

necessarily a sports coupé, but perhaps a performance hatchback, a latter-day idea along the lines of the Sport quattro. From there, the two ideas of a shorter A3 and an achievable replacement for the quattro Spyder came together. The A3C was born.

American designer Freeman Thomas – said by colleagues to be 'more German than a German' – was asked to look at the project and take it further. His initial sketches in May and June 1994 met with such approval that he was teamed with pre-development engineer Ralf-Gerhard Wilner. This would ensure that the design developed with production, and more importantly production costs, in mind. Audi could not afford, financially or politically, another quattro Spyder.

The shape of the TT, as it was to become, changed little throughout the design process. Freeman Thomas is quoted as saying of the early A3C sketches: 'This car speaks German', by which it is assumed he was referring not only to its strong styling which implies structural integrity but perhaps its rounded shape and relatively large wheels, hinting at the silver arrow racing cars of the 1930s.

Certainly the A3C took one major quality of the 1930s cars, their (then) revolutionary aerodynamic shape. It is also interesting to note also that all Freeman Thomas's sketches of the A3C, show the car in silver – perhaps he just wanted to avoid Fidji orange!

The final lesson learnt from the quattro Spyder was that its cost was not prohibitive per se, but was certainly prohibitive to build to Audi standards. This was something that was central to the A3C or TT: Audi build standards. It could not be a lightweight sports car eschewing comfort and practicality for track-driving thrills, it had to be usable. Audi was also mindful of just how wide a market the car would have, not just geographically speaking but demographically too. One of Freeman Thomas's 1994 sketches of the 'low-drag coupé' is captioned 'mature' and that the design should feel grown-up and that all age groups, men and women, should feel like 'wearing this coupé'. That 'wearing'

DID YOU KNOW?

Designer Freeman Thomas suggested Edelweiss as a name for the TT, since he wore traditional German dress to the design office, including an edelweiss in his hat band.

comment would have even greater significance once the interior came to be designed.

For now however, the TT was beginning to near its final shape. The timescale for the design of the car had been rapid to say the least and no doubt, having an existing platform to work on, and hence rigid limits set, had cut the designers freedom and hence timing. However, it had not limited the flair or style and as the car's silhouette began to form, both coupé and open cars were penned. The overall feel however was shared and in addition to visual references to the 1930s racing cars there were also hints at classic 'Bauhaus' principles.

Above: This car speaks German! An early TT concept car. (Audi Tradition)

Below: Strong and simple lines denote the TT concept's style. (Audi Tradition)

Outside forces

Over a couple of months a small team consisting of Freeman Thomas, Ralf-Gerhard Wilner and two modellers, worked in a rented studio outside of, but usefully close to, the factory at Ingolstadt. The coupé and open car – already being termed 'roadster', more commonly in English nomenclature, hinting at the designer's desire for the TT to fulfil traditional sports car values – were developed in parallel. Once these quarter-scale models had been completed they were presented to Group Chairman Ferdinand Piëch. Even at this early stage, the car had to win the approval of those at the very top of the VW-Audi Group. The model gained this acceptance and then the race was on to produce a full-size car.

Hinting at a longer rear deck reminded Audi enthusiasts of the mid-engined quattro Spyder. (Audi Tradition)

At this stage the car drew some cues from the Avus. Its rear deck had a flat section, aft of the curved shield-shaped rear window, hinting that this would be a true coupé with a lidded boot or trunk rather than a tailgate. The cabin swaged considerably at the waistline too, giving more of a 'jet fighter canopy' look to the upper section and this was a complete, elongated dome, without a flat face anywhere upon it. The frontal treatment was close to the final TT however with twin lamps, a style copied at the rear. Set into cylindrical recesses the tail lights resembled those of Ferraris or Corvettes. With a transverse engine it meant that a long traditional coupé nose was not needed here. Why make the car look as if it had a six-cylinder in-line engine when it would have (initially) a transverse four-cylinder unit? This allowed what is now termed a cab-forward design, with the passenger compartment well forward on the vehicle and allowing not only ample scope for occupants and luggage behind the driver's position, but also suggesting the lines of a mid-engined car like the quattro Spyder.

Most car design projects have a single, simple theme running through them and the TT was no different. Single it may have been – just one word – but simple it was not. Freeman Thomas used the word 'absolute', to describe the shape he strove for. 'We wanted an absolute shape, like a Leica camera for instance.' This ran through the design team, every item was analysed and the team questioned itself over and over to ensure any area of the car was 'absolute' rather than merely aesthetic, functional before it was fashionable. Ironic then, that the TT became an icon simply for its style. Perhaps function is always stronger than fashion in the automobile.

The so-called baseball-glove interior treatment stemmed from Rost's time at the American Audi Design Studio in Simi Valley, California. (Audi Tradition)

The TT's design was also about emphasis of the main elements and the wheels draw the eye more strongly in the TT's shape than virtually any other sports coupé. The TT's design was driven 'to a large extent by the wheels', Peter Schreyer has been quoted as saying. 'First of all because of the almost geometrical shape of the wheel arches and the way they stand out from the body, but also because of the way the shoulder lines follow the front and rear cut-outs, thus maintaining a close contact with the wheels. It is this design aspect above all else which gives the TT such an exceptionally compact appearance.'

Some of Freeman Thomas's earliest sketches for the A3C had proportionally even larger wheels giving virtually no depth at all in the front and rear wings over the top of the tyres. It was his biggest compliment to the design of the Avus, whose massive tyres prompted bulges in the wings front and rear to accommodate them, in the same manner as a full-bodied sports racing car. The A3C stopped short of that and the TT with its need for controllable production costs took another step back, but the feeling was still present.

After just eight weeks of refining the body shape, it was time to start on the interior. Surely if Freeman Thomas's comments on 'wearing' the car were to be realised the interior would be every bit as important as the exterior. Despite being based on the A3 platform, the interior could no more be a reworking of the A3's cabin, than the exterior could be merely a re-bodied A3. To this end Audi assigned the interior design to Romulus Rost. He was known for his thoughts on functional, even simple, design, but one with a high level of tactility and human involvement. Extensive use of aluminium combining structure and style is a keynote of the TT's interior. Rost used aluminium as this was important to Audi's technology at the time, with the advent of the A8 and the styling cues in the TT's exterior taken from the Avus. He is also quoted as saying of the interior that 'it's essential for the onlooker to gain the impression that human beings have been at work here, the leather has to smell like leather; the seams have to reveal that they were sewn by hand.' It's a view close to Romulus Rost's whole design philosophy. He is known for his love of English traditional hand-made garments, and Morgan sports cars. The 'human' element must be strong.

However, he was also very much aware of the simplicity of the TT's lines. He first saw the quarter-scale model in late Summer 1994 and was impressed by its simple shape, but one which possessed a totally unique character.

'Absolute' air vents made it through to production cars. (Spectrum Media)

Rost flew to the American Audi Design Studio in Simi Valley, California in September 1994 to work on a new seat buck, but returned just before Christmas with full-scale drawings of the entire interior. He might have been anticipating the first question that came from those who viewed them: 'Isn't the interior rather simple?'

Simply strong

This simple interior was quite deliberate. Rost wanted to use a lot of bare aluminium, not only to create a link with Audi's innovation in the use of this material in its cars, but also to mark out the TT as a sporting car. The interior should resemble that of a stripped-out

Ready for takeoff: the TTS. (Audi Tradition)

sports racing car, but Rost also had very firm ideas on its tactile qualities too. Rarely would the driver touch the aluminium, the contact points would be leather and soft-touch plastics. He had taken the 'absolute' view that Thomas had applied to the car's exterior. It had to be an absolute sports coupé, but it also had to be an absolute Audi. Tactility was important in establishing the level of quality feel and ultimately, the car's price positioning.

The interior of the car was of paramount importance to the TT. So many coupés, built essentially from the components of family cars within a given manufacturer's range, are let down by an interior that is obviously shared with more mundane models in the group. Relatively speaking, a different bodyshell is inexpensive to create, but a dedicated interior design, at relatively low volumes of production, is proportionally quite costly. The TT's interior serves one further function, it sets the TT apart from the range, despite it being based heavily on the A3. It indicates to the buyer of the car, Audi's commitment to individualism. After all, one cannot see the exterior of the car while driving it.

That is where the 'absolute' thinking enters the design process for the interior, in just the same way as the exterior. At each stage and in every detail of the design the team would ask itself if it was creating an 'absolute'. 'Are the ventilation outlets absolute, is that an "absolute headlight"?' Peter Schreyer later recalled. 'If anything fell short of this definition, we would throw it out and start again.'

The TTS shows the same styling values in open form as the TT Coupé concept. (Audi Tradition)

This extended to not allowing substitution of materials in the car. If the component was meant to look like aluminium, then quite simply it would have to be made of aluminium. What could be more logical than that, the team considered.

In March 1995, the full-size models of the Coupé exterior and an interior were completed in clay. Shortly afterwards, a further mould was made and then the roof was removed to give the first full-size representation of the Roadster.

The car at this point had changed little from the

The TT and TTS concept cars revealed in Tokyo. (Audi Tradition)

original sketches that Thomas had created, although the original side window was supplemented by a second rear three-quarter side one, to the great effect of making the interior lighter and giving it a more open feel. This would be seen in the production TT, but the concept TT would be shown with an enlarged single-window design. This one more closely matched the TTS open car concept, in that from the side elevation it looked more like a roadster with a hardtop fitted than a fixed-head coupé . However, the truth was that the A3C was penned as a fixed-head coupé in the first instance to form the TT concept and the TTS open car merely created from it.

The two cars were then engineered slightly more. The decision about the line-up of engines was taken, although at this stage the quattro four-wheel-drive system's use was not definite, from either model type or engine option standpoints. The engine itself however, was decided upon. The 20-valve 1.8-litre (110cu in) engine from the A4 would be used in 150bhp form in the TT Coupé and 219bhp in the TTS Roadster concepts.

The body would be a steel shell with all the attached panels of doors, tailgate and bonnet being in aluminium.

Once the two cars had been approved by the board of management, Freeman Thomas and Romulus Rost, travelled to Italy and Turin-based Italdesign, the company entrusted with building the two prototypes for the Frankfurt and Tokyo motor shows of 1995. The TT Coupé would be unveiled on home ground, the TTS Roadster in Tokyo. Italdesign completed the cars in just four months. Work on the Coupé had started first but the TTS open car proceeded virtually in parallel being finished by the last week of August. The Coupé was ready for the Frankfurt show in September leaving a few more man-hours for fine-tuning of the TTS before its trip to Japan. On their last night in Turin at Italdesign, Thomas and Rost celebrated with cigars. The wrappers of these were signed, dated and placed inside one of the roll-over hoops of the TTS prototype just

The long road to production saw minor changes for the final TT road-going car, not least of which is the small, rear side window. (*What Car?*)

Below and opposite: Out in the open: the two concept cars released from their design studio for photography. (Audi Tradition)

before it was finally welded into place on the car. That celebration was clearly justified since the team had achieved its goals. It had stuck to the 'absolute' doctrine yet created an individual sports coupé, and upon production-ready mechanical components.

It is only when the final car is seen, complete with its Audi badge, that the true scale of this achievement could be appreciated.

It looks like a coupé that Audi would build and it would be hard to imagine the TT wearing the badge of say a French or Italian maker; this car truly does speak German.

The prototype TT Coupé met with universal adulation from press and public alike at the Frankfurt Motor Show. The press called for the car to be built and as soon as possible, but there was no response from Ingolstadt. Of course what Audi knew, or more accurately a small group of people within Audi knew, was that the TTS open car concept would be unveiled just seven weeks later at the Tokyo show in November. Audi wanted public opinion on both prototypes before the final, but many felt inevitable, decision to produce the TT was taken.

The road to production

The two prototype cars had been built using a system the engineers called the 'map-square'. This allowed each section of the car, interior or exterior to be divided up into sections so that each one could be analysed for its technical feasibility for both production suitability and the sharing of major components between the two versions. The two prototypes shown at Frankfurt and Tokyo were drivable, but there were many more man-hours to be expended before they would become the production TT Coupé and TT Roadster.

These man-hours would culminate in the start of pre-production prototypes, 35 of which began assembly in March 1997. This was an illustration, if ever one were needed, between the rapid design, modelling and concept building process, and the much more involved engineering procedure needed to bring the cars to production readiness.

Since the TT was based on the A3 platform, the engine and major components were already in a production state, so it was the TT's unique shape that was, proportionally, to need more time to reach its road-going status.

It is due to aerodynamics that the shape of a car can change radically from the ideas penned by the original designer to the outline which is preferable for overall aerodynamic efficiency or cost of build. The TT's 'absolute' approach meant that where performance versions of family cars grew wings and spoilers – as much to emphasise their performance intentions as to give any real aerodynamic benefit – the TT would take the opposite route. Its shape was clean, devoid of spoilers and air dams. It was left to the unseen underside to do most of the aerodynamic work. The drag coefficient for the TT concept design was a creditable 0.34. The wide wheels and tyres accounted for some 25 per cent of total drag – no more than would be expected in such a car – with the requirement for large air intake openings in the car's frontal mask adding to the resistance.

Several hundred hours of wind tunnel testing proved that technology which had previously been used to good effect in grand prix racing cars could benefit the TT. Any wing or aerofoil creates drag while it meets the air at an angle in order to create a downward force upon the car. In racing this downward force is huge, but at such high speeds it has to be, since a virtually static 'wedge' of air beneath the car is trying to lift it from the track, reducing grip. This situation of wings on top of the car, trying to compensate for the lifting effect from beneath, went unchanged for decades until the late 1970s when Colin Chapman, the brilliant automotive engineer and founder of Lotus cars, discovered the 'ground effect' principle. The air beneath the car was made to reduce the lift and in lesser forms the technology found its way into road going 'super cars' in the 1980s and '90s. Audi used similar principles to good effect with huge panels beneath the front and rear sections of the TT.

Not only did these panels reduce the drag around the front and rear suspension components, themselves highly 'destructive' to the smooth ideal air flow, but reduced lift front and rear too, by use of scoop intakes in the front panel and a spoiler beneath the rear of the TT, just forward of the rear wheels. Quite early in the TT's production life however, Audi had to resort to fitting a rear spoiler on the luggage bay cover after some high-speed stability problems.

The Roadster's soft-top was to be the subject of very careful design. Not only did it have to have a good aerodynamic integrity to reduce noise and fuel consumption, but its simple linkage had to make it light enough to operate with one hand, or require only a low-energy motor for power operation.

Since the roof is a major structural area in the fixed-head coupé, the TT Roadster's body has to be fitted with additional bracing to make up for the loss of a rigid roof. The extra weight this created – allied to the slightly inferior aerodynamics – is the reason behind the original concept cars being shown with the more powerful engine fitted only to the TTS open car. However, Audi's engineers managed to keep the additional weight due to the strengthening in check. Using mainly bulkhead plates to achieve the rigidity, it accounts for only 60 per cent of the additional weight normally associated with making a convertible from a fixed-head car. It also gives the Roadster an exceptional level of torsional rigidity. This is a major contribution to the car's fine handling, since suspension engineers need a stable platform for fine tuning of the car's suspension geometry. A bodyshell which twists and bends under cornering loads means far less accurate suspension tuning can be set.

Nevertheless, the car had to remain true to the 'absolute' doctrine. The soft-top would not be lined – a folding metal roof was discounted as being too complex and not 'absolute' enough. A glass rear window is used however for the improved visibility and the roll-over hoops, although once more hinting at racing car practice, offer full occupant protection in the unlikely event of a roll-over accident.

Although the TT came before the TTS the two production cars of Coupé and Roadster were developed in parallel. Not for Audi the simple matter of chopping the top off a coupé to form an open sports car. The TT Coupé and TT Roadster must offer identical values in driver pleasure with regard to engine, chassis and dynamics. The differences between the two must be of choice, not compromise.

DID YOU KNOW?

The inspiration for the TTS Roadsters 'open-stitched' leather seats was a baseball glove. Romulus Rost spent many months at the American Audi Design Studio while penning the TT interior.

Under the skin – TT technologies

It is no exaggeration to say that Audi rewrote the rulebook for performance cars with the original quattro. Four-wheel drive had long been used for off-road vehicles and for those normally expected to operate in difficult road conditions. The military, emergency services and local authorities needed such vehicles for all-season capability. The use of four-wheel-drive vehicles by the private motorist had, until then, been limited to off-road leisure pursuits and the need for a heavy vehicle with good traction for towing a boat or a large caravan. However, all these vehicles subscribed to the same design rules. They were tall, heavy cross-country 4x4s with poor handling and performance. Although many high-performance conversions had been developed through the 1970s by independent companies, mainly on the Range Rover, the real benefits of four-wheel drive in a purely road-going vehicle were yet to be realised.

A few competition cars had been developed with four-wheel drive, but for racing the weight penalties were generally considered to cancel-out the grip benefits. For sports cars the accepted practice was to build a car with minimal weight, with that weight carried low down, stiff suspension, and wide tyres. Whether front-engined as in the traditional roadster and GT designs, mid-engined in the 1970s and '80s breed of supercars, or rear-engined in the ever-green Porsche 911, the development was the same. The front tyres took the steering loads, the rear tyres the traction loads.

Opposite: The deeper front air-dam make the V6 immediately recognisable (Audi Press)

Right: Devoid of scoops or spoilers, the TT's lines are clean. (Audi UK)

The quattro changed all that. It shared the traction load between all four tyres. This meant the suspension could be set for better ride quality and still attain sports car cornering grip and in a four-seat sports coupé, rather than a specialised sports car, this is a major consideration.

At the A3C's inception, the quattro four-wheel-drive system was considered only worthwhile in the most powerful of the planned cars. This had been Audi's original thinking for the quattro, as power and weight were increasingly overwhelming the traction capabilities of front-wheel-drive cars. However, as the A3C developed and the choice of engines became clear, so the thinking on the benefits of four-wheel drive spread to most of the range. Indeed, the very name quattro was a brand in itself by the time the TT saw the light of day and a new group of rally-inspired Japanese four-wheel-drive performance saloons was courting the

Starter motors

The quattro was written into motoring folklore for its four-wheel drive, but during its life, it did more to develop the turbocharged petrol engine, than it did the four-wheel-drive chassis. Audi had already built the five-cylinder turbo engine for the quattro and used it in the 200 Turbo saloon, and the quattro's rally exploits developed the engine in very rapid order. Audi used this knowledge through various RS and S series quattro saloons, even developing twin turbos for the V-configuration engines. The TT would be powered by the already proven but no less radical five-valves-per-cylinder 1.8-litre (108cu in) turbocharged four-cylinder engine, universally known simply as the 1.8T. The A3C was originally planned to use the 150PS 1.8 five-valve engine, but it was realised during the design of the car that this

performance car buyer. Audi might have started the whole race, but now it needed the quattro system just to get on to the starting grid.

would not give it a sufficient separation from the rest of the A3 models and establish its performance identity. So the TT quattro would be offered with two more powerful 1.8T engines at launch, in different states of tune. The 150bhp engine would however be used with front-wheel drive for an entry-level model.

DID YOU KNOW?

The unit of PS, which stands for Pferdestärke, is the metric equivalent of horsepower and is generally used by Volkswagen and Audi alongside kW, the favoured metric unit, to denote engines' outputs. In English language material, Audi simply uses the PS figure with a bhp (brake horsepower) designation. In actual fact, 1bhp is equal to 1.0139PS, but the TT 177.5bhp Coupé or 221.9bhp Roadster hardly trips off the tongue as easily as 'one-eighty' or 'two-two-five' do.

These two engines offered 180PS (132kW) and 225PS (165kW).

Both engines share the same basic layout. They displace 1,781cc (108cu in) with a bore of 81mm (3.2in) and stroke of 86.4mm (3.4in), and have five valves for each cylinder, controlled by double overhead camshafts operating hydraulic bucket-type tappets.

The 180PS engine has a 9.5:1 compression ratio and develops its 180PS output at 5,500rpm with its maximum torque of 235Nm (173lb ft) from 1,950rpm through to 5,000rpm, for maximum flexibility. This 'torque plateau' is achieved by the sophisticated breathing of the engine, through the five-valve layout and the small KKK turbocharger, a K03 unit. This is not only relatively small, allowing it to pick up speed rapidly for high boost pressures at low engine speeds, but it incorporates an air divert valve when the engine is on the overrun. This reduces the slowing of the turbo and

hence throttle response is improved, minimising 'turbo-lag', as it is commonly known.

The control of all these elements, in addition to ignition timing and fuel metering is entrusted to the Motronic 7.5 engine management system. Since the engine uses drive-by-wire – where the accelerator pedal has no mechanical link to the engine, but merely sends an accelerator position message to the Motronic unit – turbo boost can be maximised even at low engine speed and small accelerator openings. To drivers of the early quattro, where the power delivery felt as if somebody had flicked a switch at 3,000rpm, this smaller engine would be a revelation.

However, to turn the TT from a car into a range of cars, it needed an engine choice, and naturally the priority was for more power. The 225PS engine although sharing the basic design of the 180PS unit has a lower compression ratio of 9.0:1 instead of 9.5:1. The lowering of the so-called 'static' compression ratio is common practice in higher boost engines. This more powerful unit uses the slightly larger KKK turbo, the K04, and its boost pressure can reach up to 2 bar. Increasing the boost is only part of the answer and to maintain the flexibility required, the higher output engine has not one – as in the 180PS unit – but two, intercoolers. This system maintains inlet air temperatures of no more than 30°C higher than the ambient air temperature, even at full boost. In addition,

The 180PS engine seen here has one intercooler. (Audi Tradition)

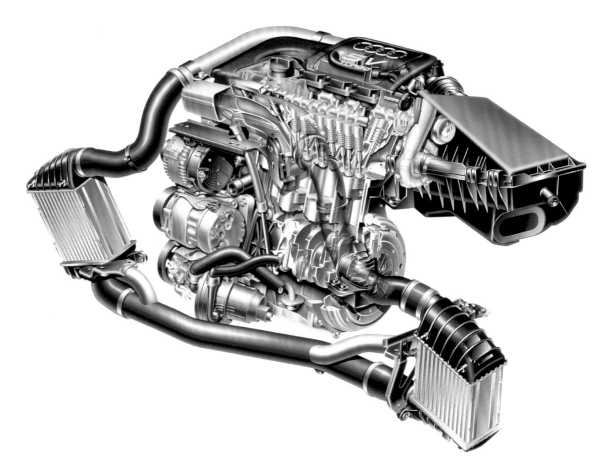

Although it differs internally, the obvious sign of a 225PS engine is its twin intercoolers. (Audi Tradition)

the exhaust and inlet manifolds are different, the air cleaner itself is larger and the internal components of piston and connecting rods are stronger, with a different dual-mass flywheel and uprated clutch completing the differences between the two engines.

The engine takes on a slightly higher revving character. The maximum output of 225PS is generated at 5,900rpm while the peak torque, albeit still spread over a wide plateau, is higher in the rev range. Some 280Nm (206lb ft) is generated from 2,200rpm to 5,500rpm.

Six appeal

Turbocharging a relatively small engine will produce one of a certain character, to create a different character you need to use a different engine. Interestingly, Freeman Thomas's earliest sketches for the A3C in March 1995 showed it with four-cylinder turbo engines in various states of tune and with the VR6, VW's classic V6 of the early 1990s. The TT would gain a narrow-angle V6 in 2003. The 3.2-litre engine displaces 3,189cc (195cu in) with an 84mm (3.3in) bore and 95.9mm (3.7in) stroke. Although not turbocharged, the 3.2 V6 has a high, 11.3:1 compression ratio. This not only gives it the output needed for it to top the TT's engine range

but a high level of fuel efficiency also. The angle of just 15° between the cylinder banks makes the unit particularly compact and suited to the TT's engine bay.

A dual-branch variable exhaust system utilises a flap which the Motronic management opens or shuts depending on engine speed, creating an exhaust note that is characterful at higher engine revolutions for a sporting note, but without being unnecessarily intrusive in city driving and at cruising speeds.

Maximum output is 250PS at 6,300 rpm with the peak torque of 320Nm (236lb ft) being available from 2,800rpm to 3,200rpm. The engine has four valves for each of its six cylinders and uses roller cam followers in place of bucket-style tappets upon which the double overhead camshafts operate. It is an indication as to how important a market the UK is to the TT, that Audi chose to launch the right-hand-drive 3.2V6 TT Coupé first, in July 2003, before the left-hand-drive model – as would normally be the case for a German manufacturer.

Audi also introduced to the UK market, a TT at the opposite end of the power scale, alongside the 3.2V6. A 150PS version of the four-cylinder 1.8T engine was offered to make an entry-level Roadster to compete with the growing band of sporting-style cars whose buyers do not need high performance as they are driven almost entirely in city traffic, but who appreciate the finer points of the TT's design.

The narrow-angle V6 fits neatly into the TT's engine bay. (Audi UK)

Identical to the 180PS engine in bore, stroke, displacement and compression ratio it produces 150PS at 5,700rpm. Peak torque stands at 210Nm (155lb ft) and is available from 1,750rpm to 4,600rpm. The TT 150PS employs a five-speed transmission providing front-wheel drive, rather than the quattro four-wheel-drive system, reflecting the design team's original view on the engine output being related to the number of driven wheels. For the enthusiast however, the 150PS front-drive TT is somewhat half-hearted.

Initially, the 180PS TT was offered with a five-speed transmission while the 225PS engine had a six-speed unit. Later in the TT's life the 180PS gained the six-speed transmission too. While the five-speed units are conventional two-shaft gearboxes, the six-speed manual is a three-shaft design. This additional third shaft handles fifth, sixth and reverse ratios, and compared with the two-shaft gearbox it offers a more compact design which is suited to the TT's short-nose styling and hence packaging requirements. Despite taking up less room the six-speed manual unit is still capable of transmitting 350Nm (258lb ft).

However, the 3.2-litre V6 TT is noted for its ground-breaking six-speed DSG (direct-shift gearbox) – a unique type of automatic transmission unit.

Direct control

The DSG unit has been designed to offer all the advantages of a sporting close-ratio manual gearbox combined with a quick shifting automatic transmission, with none of the negative aspects of either. The selector looks like any other Audi automatic selector lever, with its additional miniature Tiptronic gate for manual overriding shifts, and naturally, there is no clutch pedal. It is not a conventional automatic with a fluid coupling, but uses traditional friction clutch material, the same as a manual transmission. The design features twin automated clutches, permitting exceptionally rapid (0.02-second) manual gear changes via the gear lever or steering wheel paddles, yet it can also behave like a traditional automatic shift for more relaxed urban driving.

The basis for the new DSG is the six-speed manual gearbox capable of handling up to 350Nm (258lb ft) of torque.

The technology of this twin-clutch transmission has its roots in the quattro's rallying heyday. As far back as 1985, Walter Röhrl successfully tested it in the Audi Sport quattro S1, its electronics at the time were not always able to withstand the extreme heat and vibration that rallying threw at them, but the principle of the gearbox was successful.

The DSG virtually eliminates the break in power flow that is normally unavoidable when the clutch is disengaged to operate a conventional manual shift gearbox. The next higher or next lower gear is already pre-engaged before it is selected at the gear lever or shift paddle, so that no interruptions occur under hard acceleration during gear changing.

Integrated twin multi-plate clutches with sophisticated electronic control enable two gears to be engaged at the same time. With any given gear engaged, as the next gearshift point is approached, the appropriate gear is pre-selected, but its clutch remains disengaged. The gearshift process opens the clutch of the current gear and closes the clutch of the new gear at the same time. The gear change takes place under load, with the result that a permanent flow of power is maintained.

Above: The DSG's selector looks like that of any conventional automatic. (Audi UK)

Below left: DSG transmission was first applied to the awesome Sport S1 quattro rally car in the mid-1980s. (Audi UK)

Below right: The DSG can operate on 'D', 'S' or manual Tiptronic, like a conventional Audi automatic transmission. (Spectrum Media)

Opposite above: In first gear (red) with second gear (green) already selected.

Opposite below: The first gear clutch (red) opens and the second gear clutch (green) closes, to make the shift.

Audi TT 3.2 quattro

with the new Direct Shift Gearbox DSG
Operating principle, acceleration in 1st gear

02/03

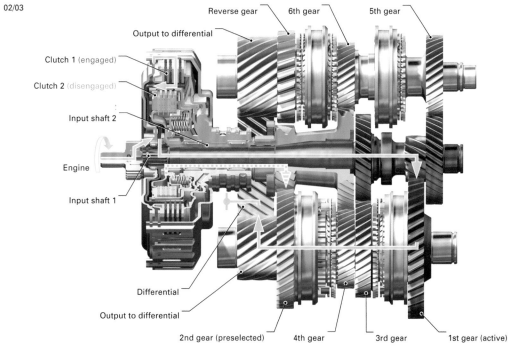

Reverse gear

6th gear

5th gear

Output to differential

Clutch 1 (engaged)

Clutch 2 (disengaged)

Input shaft 2

Engine

Input shaft 1

Differential

Output to differential

2nd gear (preselected)   4th gear   3rd gear   1st gear (active)

Audi TT 3.2 quattro

with the new Direct Shift Gearbox DSG
Operating principle, acceleration in 2nd gear

02/03

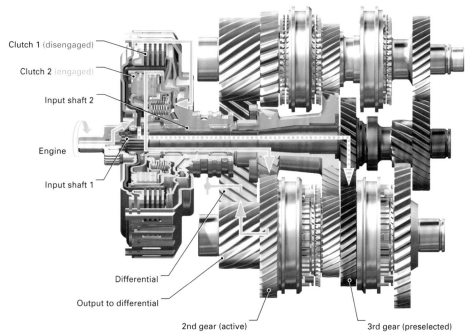

Clutch 1 (disengaged)

Clutch 2 (engaged)

Input shaft 2

Engine

Input shaft 1

Differential

Output to differential

2nd gear (active)   3rd gear (preselected)

There are three operating modes. Selecting 'D' provides traditional automatic gearshifts, then 'S' mode, in which upshifts are retarded, downshifts advanced and the shifting process accelerated, and finally, manual override. Here, the driver can choose the gear selected by means of the gear lever in the manual gate or the shift paddles on the steering wheel, which are standard with the DSG transmission. These paddles also temporarily engage the manual shift function, even in automatic D and S modes.

Like a conventional manual gearbox, DSG transmission ratios are present on input and auxiliary shafts, but in contrast to the manual gearbox, the input shaft is divided into two sections – a hollow outer shaft, and an inner shaft. The first, third, fifth and reverse gears are located on the inner shaft and the hollow shaft handles the even-numbered gears.

Each shaft is selected by means of a separate multi-plate clutch running in oil. The two electronically controlled, hydraulically actuated clutches are packed inside each other and can be controlled in such a way that every conceivable form of pulling away is possible, from a gentle start-off on slippery surfaces to Formula 1-style 'launch control' acceleration at full throttle.

Special solenoid-operated valves regulate the application pressure of the two clutches. The electronics process signals from ten individual sensors, to calculate which additional gear is to be pre-selected by the corresponding positioning cylinder and selector forks. With the DSG transmission, the TT offers the response and fuel economy of a manual transmission, with the convenience of an automatic. It ideally suits the nature

Top: Paddles can be used for manual shifts . . .

Above: . . . and are mounted on the steering wheel, not the column, and turn with it. (Both Spectrum Media)

Right: Lateral thinking. The TT's engine is mounted transversely and needs a different quattro system from other Audis. (Audi Tradition)

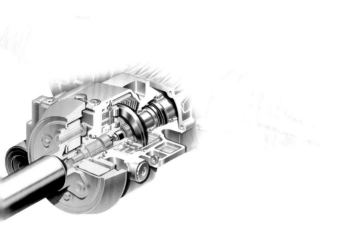

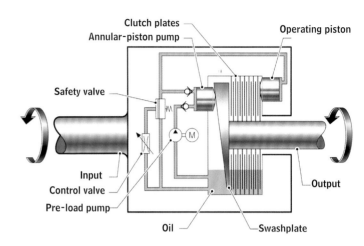

The Swedish Haldex coupling – mounted at the rear – is the key to the TT's four-wheel-drive system. (Audi Tradition)

The Haldex coupling gives drive to the rear wheels as the front ones begin to spin. (Audi Tradition)

of the TT and its persona as the sophisticated approach to the sports car genre.

Quattro by another name

The TT was the first Audi to use a compact quattro four-wheel-drive system, which is different from the original quattro – and all other Audi quattros except the A3 as they all use a longitudinally positioned engine. The drive can be taken through a conventional centre differential as the gearbox is in line with the car's length, but in the TT, which has a transverse engine layout, the gearbox is located across the car.

The answer for the TT came from within the VW-Audi family. The TT's system is better known as 4MOTION and is used by the VW Golf in its four-wheel-drive guise. The key to the system is the Swedish, Haldex coupling which is positioned just ahead of the rear differential. Its function is to drive the rear wheels should the front wheels begin to lose grip. In effect, while driving on a dry road in a straight line, the TT's engine is only supplying torque to its front wheels.

The Haldex unit is a coupling, not a centre differential like the Torsen unit or earlier lockable unit. It can only ever supply torque to the four wheels in the ratio of 100 per cent to the front and zero to the rear through to 50 per cent to the front and 50 to the rear, or any point in between. A Torsen differential could, in certain circumstances, supply up to 75 per cent of its torque to the rear wheels. The Haldex coupling never creates a torque bias to the rear. As a rule of thumb, this is the test to

determine if a four-wheel-drive system uses a true centre differential, or a torque transferring coupling.

This means that the handling balance of the TT differs from earlier quattros. However, the very fact that the Haldex coupling is mounted at the rear, assists in creating a more even weight distribution than the early nose-heavy quattros experienced, with their 'centre' differential housed within the main transmission unit under the bonnet.

To maintain the handling response expected of a sports car, the coupling was developed with Haldex specifically for the TT and is quick acting to say the least. The heart of the coupling is a multiple set of clutch plates, which run in oil but this does not have any driving effect as the Haldex does not operate like the viscous coupling found in the earlier VW Syncro system, which Audi has never used.

The clutches act conventionally to transfer torque from the coupling's input shaft – which is the output of the final drive unit at the front wheels – to its output shaft, which drives the rear wheels. The clutches are acted upon by hydraulic pressure from an electrically driven pre-load pump and an annular-piston actuating pump which is driven by a swashplate. This swashplate is affected as a difference occurs in rotational speeds between the front and rear wheels. Since the swashplate itself is mounted on the coupling's output shaft – the drive to the rear wheels – this difference in rotation causes it to engage with piston valves controlling the flow of the pre-load pump. This allows pressure to the clutch plates engaging them and transmitting drive progressively to the rear wheels. The amount of torque the clutch plates transfer is infinitely variable allowing anywhere from zero to 50 per cent of the available torque to be transmitted to the rear wheels.

The process begins when there is just 45° of difference in the rotational position of the front and rear drive portions of the coupling. In real terms this means that the coupling starts to transfer torque to the rear when the TT has travelled just 250mm (10in) along the road!

The pre-load pump and its valves take electronic input as well as the rotational speed differential input from the swashplate. This means that the coupling is not only able to respond to the requirements of the DSG transmission launch control, but is also fully compatible with the ABS and ESP systems.

The mixing of ABS and four-wheel drive was once considered an alchemist's art. The original quattro disabled its ABS when the centre differential was locked, since ABS cannot operate effectively with two or more wheels mechanically locked together. The downside of this fact is that road conditions where the driver would need to lock the centre differential, would be the exact conditions where ABS would be a great comfort. This was the main reason behind the later Ur quattros having a Torsen centre differential; it allowed the ABS to function fully.

The TT's system needs to allow not only the ABS and EDL – more on which later – but the ESP system, to operate correctly. A simple override process disengages the clutch pack in the Haldex coupling when the ABS circuit begins to function so that the TT quattro effectively becomes front-wheel drive allowing the ABS to function unhindered by any torque transfer. The ESP system, which applies the brake to a single wheel or diagonally opposite wheels – to correct the car's line in a slippery corner, can operate with the Haldex unit as there is no locking or active torque transfer across either the front or rear wheel pairs. Where older quattros used a locking rear differential and the early V8 quattro used a Torsen rear differential – both of which would have hindered ESP systems if they had been around at the time – the TT uses the EDL system.

EDL (electronic differential lock) is something of a misnomer since it is not a differential lock at all! The EDL system is simply the VW-Audi Group's term for what is generally known as electronic traction control. It works in conjunction with the ABS system using the

ABS sensors which constantly monitor the rotational speed of each wheel. Where the ABS system releases the brake on a wheel which is rotating slower than the others (starting to lock) the EDL does the opposite; it applies the brake to a wheel that is turning faster than the others (starting to spin). This can best be seen by a two-wheel drive car with one front wheel on wet grass or mud at the side of the road, and the other on the road surface. A conventional differential will merely spin the wheel on the mud and waste the torque, with the car struggling to drive away. The EDL system brakes this wheel equalising the load on either side of the differential, to make the differential respond in the same way as if both wheels were on the road. Place this system on all four wheels, then combine it with the TT's four-wheel-drive coupling, and the resulting traction is impressive to say the least.

Geometry class

Four-wheel drive in itself does not make for a fine handling car. It might provide impressive traction from a standstill or out of slow, tight corners, but the TT's suspension must follow proven sports car values. Naturally however, the Audi design team did not follow convention too closely.

The front suspension although employing a quite conventional MacPherson spring strut features a lower wishbone geometry to make the lower suspension compact, but also capitalises on the low centre of gravity and wide, 1,527mm (60in) front track. Although the Haldex coupling is mounted in the rear, the TT still has a frontal weight bias, so the anti-roll capability is particularly important. The engineers used a 1:1 anti-roll bar ratio. This means that every bit of spring compression is transferred into a rotational force upon the anti-roll bar. The TT has no roll which goes unchecked and hence its anti-roll performance is linear with spring travel. This not only assists in reducing roll and weight transfer but also improves steering capability and feel. From the A3's basic suspension the TT has modified settings for camber and toe-out. Under large suspension compressions the front suspension adopts a moderate toe-out stance. This assists in neutral handling and in braking

Opposite top: The Roadster shares all the safety technology you would expect in a fixed-roof car. (Audi Tradition)

Opposite bottom: The TT's front suspension, showing the drive shafts but with the transaxle missing for clarity. (Audi Tradition)

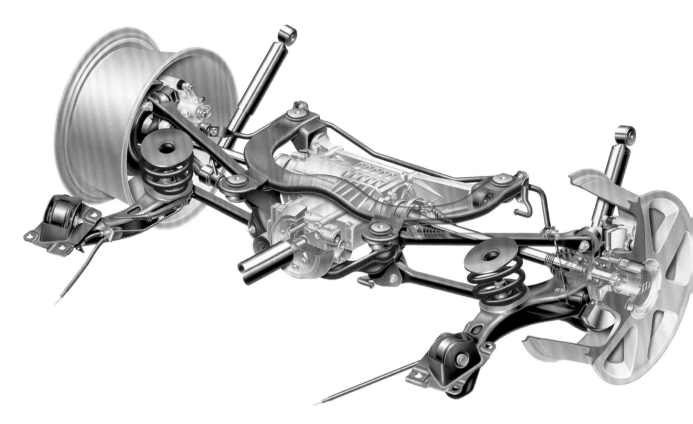

Above: The rear suspension of a TT quattro. The Haldex coupling is the brake drum-shaped device just ahead of the rear differential casing. (Audi Tradition)

stability, itself of great importance in such a short wheelbase design, particularly one with the acceleration of the TT.

The rear suspension differs slightly between the front-wheel-drive TT and TT quattro although the basics are the same, with trailing arms and long-radius double wishbones. Unlike the MacPherson strut system employed at the front, the rear springs and dampers are separated. The rear springs are much shorter than the front ones, and operate just forward of the rear wheel centres on the end of the trailing arms. The dampers are mounted at a considerable angle of incline, just behind the rear wheel centres, to maintain the low profile.

The bushing compliance in the rear suspension has been carefully tuned to avoid rear-steer characteristics that can plague trailing-arm systems, particularly when the driver suddenly lifts from the accelerator in mid-bend.

Where the front-wheel-drive TT's rear suspension has its anti-roll bar mounted directly on the simple torsion beam axle, the TT quattro's anti-roll bar is connected to

the hubs by separate operating rods. This is to allow clearance of the rear differential and its associated components.

The requirements of the EDL and ESP place further loading on the braking components, in addition to the expected task of slowing a high-performance car. The TT's brakes are reassuringly strong. The front discs are ventilated 312mm (12.3in) diameter items with 256mm (10.1in) diameter units at the rear, which are solid on the lower engine output models but ventilated on the 225PS engine.

The 3.2-litre V6 car has a different braking system. Borrowed from the RS4 quattro it boasts 334mm (13.1in) diameter ventilated discs at the front and 256mm (10.1in) diameter vented discs at the rear, with floating callipers.

All TT's feature EBD (electronic brakeforce distribution) to ensure the maximum force is applied to all wheels no matter what weight distribution or loadings are acting upon the car at the time.

The final system in which the brakes play a part is the ESP. This takes a huge amount of information to establish the state of the car and its attitude at any given time. Sensors measure road and individual wheel speeds, applied steering angle, lateral acceleration – the sideways forces trying to push the car off the outside of a corner – and yaw rate. Yaw rate is the angular velocity of the car about the vertical axis, which is in effect the rate at which the car is trying to spin around, for instance when the rear end of the car begins to slide wide in a corner, or the front pushes-on into understeer. The ESP system measures all these parameters and can apply or release individual brakes, reduce the engine power, and operate in conjunction with the EDL system to try to prevent the driver from losing control. The ESP is particularly effective in a sudden avoidance manoeuvre at speed as the system can react more quickly than even the most skilled driver to bring the car back into line.

Of course, all the TT's traction and stability systems rely on four final components: the tyres. Although the original sketches of the A3C showed it to have wheels of 20in or so, with very low profile tyres, they can make for a harsh ride. This might be fine for a track-biased sports car, or for the owner to make as an aftermarket choice, but the TT had to have a wheel and tyre combination able to do justice to the refinement expected of an Audi, in addition to the excitement expected of a sports car.

On the 150PS front-wheel-drive TT and the 180PS quattro, 16in alloy wheels with 205/55 R 16 tyres are used. The 225PS quattro and 3.2V6 quattro models use 17in alloy wheels shod with 245/45 R 17 tyres.

By the standards of some performance cars, the tyres might seem only moderately wide, but with the traction benefits of sharing the engine's torque through all four wheels, they need not be over wide, or need to be of varying widths front to rear – as is common with most rear-drive sports cars – making replacement an easier proposition.

The tyre choice reflects the doctrine which runs through all the TT's technologies. Every area of the car's development is to a goal, and a realisation of it. The engine choices, the traction of the quattro system, all the electronics within the stability controls and the use of passive suspension geometry. It all follows the 'absolute' thinking of the original design team. There is no technology merely for show. If it is part of the TT it is there for performance, safety or driver reward.

Below: Suspension components are highlighted in this full-car image. (Audi Tradition)

Chapter **Four**

One theme, several embodiments

From the very outset, it was clear that the TT's design team was considering the car as a complete range of models, not as a single design, differentiated merely through subtle trim and specification variations. Although never officially voiced, it is reasonable to assume that the team looked to the iconic German sports and GT car, the Porsche 911, as an indication of where the TT would need to go in terms of creating a range for itself. After all, the TT design already boasted two-wheel-drive and four-wheel-drive versions, a coupé and an open car, and if the initial designs were to be carried through, there would even be sporting versions of the car. These would be specialist models for the enthusiast to drive on the road and possibly compete on circuits at weekends. Porsche had used its Carrera and RS derivatives to create such an impression and as public 'track days' started to become a popular and accessible format for performance car drivers, the TT might be able to ride the new wave of true sports car renaissance.

As early as March 1995, Freeman Thomas had sketched four versions of the A3 Coupé, as it was then known. The first two were to become the TT itself, a coupé and a roadster design, the latter two drew inspiration from cars such as the Porsche Speedster having a lower windscreen and overall heights with a Spyder style of a removable centre roof section, and a fixed-head low-drag coupé. Thomas noted that these latter two would be specially built by Audi Sport as specialist highlights to the range.

If four different body derivatives were not enough, then the engine and drivetrain line up was even more complex. The two 'standard' models were intended to

have a four-cylinder engine in 125PS or turbocharged 150PS guises, this almost certainly was meant to be the 1.8T engine, which did of course make it into the final car. The other was the Volkswagen VR6 narrow-angle V6 engine with an intended 200PS. The two special Audi Sport versions were intended to be powered by a four-cylinder engine in turbocharged form with 230PS or the VR6 once more in 230PS form.

The driveline configuration had already set the scene for the project team's thoughts of four-wheel drive only being offered in the high-powered cars. The two Audi Sport cars were both quattros, with 230PS but the others would only feature four-wheel drive on the VR6

The Coupé was the first TT to be sketched . . .

Opposite: The number plate says it all for this 180PS Roadster. (Audi Press)

Above: . . . but the Roadster was not far behind it. (Both Audi Tradition)

Below: The rare, optional hardtop fitted to a Roadster. It looks just like the TT concept, with no second side window. (Audi Tradition)

versions, and possibly the turbo 150PS car. As it turned out, many of these initial ideas were carried through to the final production cars.

Six pack

Although Audi and Volkswagen share engines, and indeed car platforms as a whole, the VR6 in its original form never made it into the TT, or any other Audi for that matter. The design attributes of a narrow-angle V6 were however to spread right through the high performance versions of both Audi and Volkswagen front-wheel-drive cars and into the four-wheel-drive versions. This, in the A3 and TT or VW Golf cases, meant the Haldex coupling system, badged as quattro in the Audis and 4MOTION in the VWs. The V6 finally found its way into the TT in 3.2-litre (195cu in) form, its 250PS being very close to those initial design thoughts on the 230PS car.

Although different versions of the car have been introduced to different markets at different times – some markets, such as the UK, would not receive the 150PS two-wheel-drive Roadster until well into the car's life, it was the two turbo four-cylinder engines which set the scene for the TT in 1999.

However, Audi was not content to merely differentiate the cars on engine output. The 225PS car was different in several respects, not least of which was its use of the six-speed transmission. This was primarily to gain best performance from the torque curve of the 225PS engine. Although this produces a greater peak torque it is less flexible than the 180PS engine and the six-speed gear-box gains the best from it. Also, the pricing structure of the range made a premium car out of the 225PS in Roadster form – the TTS concept car was the more powerful of the two prototypes – setting the top end of the TT range. The most powerful engine combined with

Above: The Roadster with hardtop. (Audi Tradition)

Below: Later glory was to come with the 3.2-litre engine, originally considered in VR6 form. (Audi UK)

the soft-top body style set the TT up as a true high-performance Roadster in the traditional mould, albeit with very untraditional performance values.

To this end, in February 2000, Audi undertook a major recall of the TT, albeit as an option. The TT had undergone minor specification enhancements at the end of 1999, the biggest of which was the fitting of ESP as standard. However, a considerable number of early TTs had been built without the ESP system. Several high-profile accidents had made the headlines in Germany and owners of TTs without ESP feared for the resale value of their car as much as any dynamic shortcomings. Audi acted quickly, retrofitting ESP on a specially built line within the factory at Ingolstadt. Audi charged the same as the price increase the previous year for an ESP-equipped car, and provided customers with a loan car while the fitting was carried out.

To counter stories of the TT's ultimate safety or predictability Audi commissioned TÜV Süddeutschland

(South German Technical Inspection Association) to assess the TT's handling behaviour. The TÜV's summary concluded: 'The Audi TT – including its original versions – is, compared with the competition, a better-than-average sports car and is in keeping with the state of the art.'

Above: The 150PS engine has no external badging relating to its power output. (Spectrum Media)

Top right: The increased aerodynamic aids were in answer to safety fears. This is the larger spoiler on the rear of a 3.2-litre TT. (Spectrum Media)

Above right: The increased speed offered by the 3.2-litre requires a deeper front spoiler too. (Spectrum Media)

DID YOU KNOW?

In July 2000, Audi reduced the price of the TT by 10 per cent in its largest market, the UK, in the face of competition from other sports cars, while customers opting for the sports suspension with higher ride height get an allowance from the price of their TT 3.2 quattro. Also, Audi refunded TT customers when the S-Line options package became standard equipment.

Dr Franz-Josef Paefgen, chairman of the board of management of Audi AG, at the time went on record at a Munich press conference saying: 'I wish to apologise formally to our TT customers for the uncertainty which has emerged in the last few months. Our offensive is intended to put an end to this uncertainty.'

Six shift

For the 2001 model year the six-speed gearbox became standard for all TT quattros, as the requirement to upgrade the car and to keep one eye on the competition became more apparent.

The extra gear enabled the lower ratios to be spaced more closely, resulting in keener engine response for the 180PS car and – more importantly – improved mid-range performance for better overtaking performance. All this was achieved without any sacrifice in fuel consumption since the engine speed was cut at motorway speeds. It also made long-distance cruising a more relaxed affair, increasing the feeling of sophistication.

Audi was also keenly aware of the TT being something that the buyer would 'wear' and not just drive. Along with the mechanical change to standard fitment of the six-speed gearbox, a new range of colours was set to increase the TT's visual impact. Although not something which the TT lacked, many customers were keen to underline the car's style statement further. Available to special order at an extra cost, Audi added Merlin Purple for those who really wished to stand out from the crowd, and Imola Yellow, which not only harked back to Italian sports cars of the 1960s but in Germany at least had been a popular shade for aftermarket Mercedes-Benz performance conversions, and BMW's M3 was to wear a similar colour. For Audi it was a long way from the racing Auto Unions – although it would call its forthcoming new metallic silver hue, Avus.

The new gearbox bolstered the specification of the 180PS TT quattro which already included 16in alloy wheels, remote-control central locking, leather upholstered front sports seats and electronic climate control, with airbags for the driver, front passenger and the front sides. This was Audi's doctrine for the car. The interior with its bare aluminium and a simple layout, which was almost stark in places, bellied what was in fact a true GT car in the strictest sense. The sacrifices in comfort for sports car motoring had been consigned to the history books. When the TT entered the market, it quite simply required every other manufacturer to raise its game.

For Audi this level of quality was not novel, it was an expectation of the brand and of the way it built any of its cars. Audi also knew that there was scope for limited editions too. The Sport quattro of 1985 had shown this. It was built in limited numbers merely to allow it to enter international rallies under the Group B banner, but since that time, limited-edition sports and performance cars had proved popular with those seeking exclusivity.

Audi knew 'TT' would become a brand in itself just like quattro. It is the only badge on the rear of the entry-level Roadster. (Spectrum Media)

S is for special

With exclusivity in mind, the TT S-Line was created. The UK was a major target market for such a car, and by a fitting coincidence it would receive just 200 examples, the same number as required to homologate the Sport quattro. That would speak volumes to long-standing quattro enthusiasts.

The S-Line was the first ever special edition of the TT. Based on the 225PS Coupé, the Audi TT quattro S-Line was recognised externally by two exclusive paint colours and larger, 18in, nine-spoke alloy wheels, which filled their arches even more fully due to modified sports suspension lowering this version by an additional 20mm compared with the standard car.

To complement the new Misano Red or Avus Silver paintwork, the TT S-Line was available with either the familiar black leather interior, or with a unique Brilliant Red or Silver Grey leather trim, and a six-disc CD autochanger, while a BOSE sound system upgrade was also part of the S-Line interior package. At the time of introduction the special package added around 2.5 per cent to the price of the standard S-Line car but it proved so popular that Audi withdrew it from the options list – and made it standard.

For 2002, all TT models in the UK were equipped with the 18in, nine-spoke alloy wheels, with 225/40 ZR18 tyres, and the sports suspension, lowering all TT quattros compared with the original car. Model differentiation came in the form of titanium headlamp surrounds to embellish the frontal mask of the 225PS Coupé and Roadster models. The 225PS models also added xenon headlamps with washers and automatic range adjustment and a driver's information system (DIS), in the facia binnacle.

In addition, the range of standard metallic and pearl-effect paints, which were originally available at extra cost, were now offered free of charge, while the special-order colours of Avus Silver and Misano Red had their cost reduced.

Inside the TT, the two previous special order leather colours – silver and red – were made available for a nominal option price.

In spite of this equipment upgrade to S-Line levels, prices for the 2002 model year TT quattros remained unchanged.

This left Audi UK with something of a problem. Its exclusive, higher-cost S-Line car was now the standard TT. Many manufacturers might have thought little more of it, but Audi took a rather unusual step. Since the

Cold comfort: Audi offered heated seats on leather options. (Spectrum Media)

The four-cylinder cars carry no badging to differentiate their power. Only the V6 has its designation proclaimed on the TT's rear. (Spectrum Media)

specification enhancements were worth as much as 10 per cent of the previous standard car's price, TT customers with cars already on order which would not have the new equipment levels were contacted individually by their dealer to offer goodwill packages, while existing owners of the TT S-Line models were contacted and offered full reimbursement for the cost of the additional specification that had now become standard. Not a common practice in the motor industry!

The increase in equipment levels kept the TT at the head of the pack. The sports car market was undergoing something of a renaissance and the TT – or rather its success – was attracting a good deal of competition to the sector.

Its leading position was recognised soon after the S-Line package had become standard issue. One of the UK's most influential motoring magazines, *What Car?* awarded the TT its 'Best Coupé' award. This was not the first time the magazine had honoured the TT. Indeed, the 2002 honour meant that the TT quattro took away the prize for an exceptional fourth successive year. Moreover, the car that had been judged for this award was made before the announcement of the specification revisions.

Minor changes

It is an indication of the TT design's longevity that the car, despite specification enhancements, had never undergone a facelift, and when the time came, Audi even made a joke of the fact. It was the UK motor show in October 2002 that Audi chose to unveil changes to the TT's exterior, slight though they were. The UK was deliberately chosen for this, and for good reason. At that time the UK was by far the TT's most successful market. Since the Coupé first went on sale in the UK in July 1999, over 21,000 had been bought.

Audi UK hailed the unveiling as the 'the hardest exterior change to spot at the Motor Show'. Its announcement to the press was equally tongue-in-cheek as the issued statement read: *'The most visually elusive exterior improvement made to any car on show at the British International Motor Show belongs to the Audi TT quattro. The sole exterior revision is a mildly altered radiator grille, which can be seen for the first time in Britain at the NEC.'*

A serious point was being made behind this rather flippant admission. The TT had not been changed, since it simply did not require changing. Audi knew that carrying out nothing more than detail improvements would make the car a far better ownership proposition too. Not only would it have a more linear residual value standing, but owners would be more inclined to upgrade to another TT, safe in the knowledge that nothing radical would change to 'age' their pride and

Audi UK made a joke at the British Motor Show of the only improvement being a new grille, but it ushered in the V6 soon after. (Audi UK)

The V6 cars sported bigger spoilers both front and rear. (Audi UK)

joy. This was one fashion icon that would never look 'last season'.

'Audi has clearly discovered a hugely successful formula with the exceptional styling of the TT, and I can understand why the designers were reluctant to attempt any significant changes to a sports car that our customers widely regard as perfect,' commented Audi UK Director Kevin Rose, at the time.

There was a significant change to come to the TT in July 2003 however. The TT 3.2 Coupé quattro and TT 3.2 Roadster quattro used the most powerful TT engine so far, in conjunction with the DSG (direct-shift gearbox) transmission. For the first time the 150PS front-wheel-drive TT Roadster was also offered in the UK. A further

indication as to the importance of the UK as the TT's biggest market, was that the V6 cars were launched in right-hand-drive in the UK, around a month before they were launched in Germany. To complement the DSG, in July 2004 a conventional torque-converter Tiptronic automatic with six speeds, was added to the options list on the 180PS Coupé version.

To the power of six
The TT 3.2 quattro is most easily recognised by its standard, seven-spoke 18in alloy wheels, while the four-cylinder TT quattros use nine-spoke designs of the same diameter although these are available as an option for the 3.2. The aerodynamic styling package gives the V6-engined cars a slightly more aggressive look, with a low front airdam and boot-mounted spoiler. Under the

The narrow-angle 3.2-litre V6 is derived from the Volkswagen VR6, originally planned for the A3C from the earliest design stages. (Spectrum Media)

skin these 3.2-litre derivatives have a revised sports suspension package which differs from the four-cylinder cars' S-Line inspired lowered suspension. There is also the option on the TT 3.2 of the standard sports suspension which lifts the ride height to the same level as the 150PS front-wheel-drive Roadster. It is useful in creating a little more ground clearance, for cars which need to access steep ramps on a regular basis. Opting for this suspension set-up brings a small allowance in pricing to make up for deletion of the 'standard' low suspension from the specification.

Although all Audi TT models use a MacPherson strut-type front suspension and the rear is a space-efficient combined trailing and double lateral control arm arrangement, the TT 3.2 quattro models feature a special suspension set-up. This has tailored spring and damper settings with further reinforced anti-roll bars to handle the higher torque forces at work combined with high cornering speeds. The V6 engine also increases the mass upon the front suspension. This engine shares the twin-tailpipe exhaust design of the 225PS car, so the TT 3.2V6 need not stand out from the rest of the range if the owner so desires.

Braking is also uprated compared with that of the four-cylinder cars, a 17in dual-piston brake system adapted from the version used by the RS 4 guarantees the stopping power.

Of course, the TT is very much about style and Audi has created a wide range of exterior colours and interior options which can be tailored to match the car's external appearance. The interior choices begin with an Alcantara/leather combination while a moccasin-style leather is available to recreate the TTS concept car's baseball glove effect. This appeals to owners who might not want to go down the route of modifying the car after purchase, but wish to personalise their TT as much as possible. It also satisfies a sense of belonging with the history and development of the original TTS concept.

For those who require a more extrovert look there is always the factory-option of red or silver colours in Audi's smoothest Silk Nappa leather. However, the personalisation process does not end there. The Audi Exclusive Programme available through your local Audi Centre multiplies the options for exterior colour and interior trim. The programme is under continual development and with so many combinations available, no two TTs are ever likely to be exactly the same.

An Audi experience

There are several options available to TT owners which are not fitted to the car. These are the events forming the Audi Driving Experience. Using racing circuits, test-tracks and snow-covered roads these courses aim to give drivers the chance to learn and practice high-speed driving and accident avoidance techniques in a safe environment, utilise Audi's quattro and electronic safety systems, and above all, improve their awareness and skills in emergency situations.

In early 2004, Audi brought the Driving Experience programme to the UK. It had been in operation for six years in Germany and utilises both the Hockenheim Grand Prix circuit and the legendary Nürburgring the most demanding racing circuit in the world. The grand prix circuit in Barcelona is also used, along with snow driving exercises in Austria and Finland.

The UK event is held at Silverstone, and together with 'introductory' events in Europe, serves as entry to the higher levels including driving at the Nürburgring and in snowy conditions. This differentiates the Audi Driving Experience from some other manufacturer-supported driving courses as it builds on each previous event; the more events you participate in, the higher your skill

The V6 engine and DSG were launched in right-hand-drive form first. (Audi UK)

Above: Lapping at speed in the TT. (Audi Driving Experience)

Opposite: On the right track – the Audi Driving Experience offers another dimension to TT ownership. (Audi Tradition)

level becomes, and you won't find yourself covering old ground.

Naturally, Audi uses some of its most powerful cars for these events. The TT is represented by the Coupé quattro 3.2V6 with DSG transmission, while other quattros in the form of the S4 and RS6 Avant, complete the fleet.

The morning briefing is not the often-experienced 'classroom' session. The participants do not have their intelligence insulted, and the instructors – all former race or rally drivers from Germany – assume that anyone taking the course will have a good basic knowledge of car dynamics.

Six disciplines make up this one-day course, all aimed at improving driver safety and reactions, but also showing just how the Audi technologies can assist the driver in real-world on-the-road emergencies.

Since all road cars are designed to understeer upon

entering a bend too quickly, the effect of understeer and how to react to it and reduce it, is the first exercise. It's a good mental exercise to start the day too. Initially, it is difficult to throw the car into the bend too quickly when all your experience tells you not to. This is something that occurs throughout the course. You will find yourself and the car in situations you would not normally be in. How else can you learn a new skill?

Many accidents occur when drivers assume that the car cannot achieve a manoeuvre, in effect, they give up. The high speed braking and avoidance exercise soon dispels such doubts. This dramatic test involves accelerating – at full throttle in 'Sport' mode – a 450bhp RS6 Avant down a 'lane' of cones whose end is blocked. At little more than five car lengths before the wall of cones – and travelling at over 60mph – you literally

DID YOU KNOW?

Audi's Exclusive Programme, which is under constant revision, offers leather to hint at the TTS concept car's baseball glove interior.

stamp on the brake pedal to engage ABS and brake-assist, before steering into next 'lane' – braking fully the whole time – to avoid a collision. A classic emergency situation on a busy motorway or dual-carriageway. Afterwards, you can only think of one thing. How would you do that in a car without ABS, particularly when, on the road, the short reaction time is real, not simply created by forcing yourself to stay off the brakes.

The course is designed not to show the limits of tyres and electronic systems, but to allow you, as a driver, to find and then increase your own personal limits. A timed slalom in the TT is a good way to do this. It's a whole lot of fun too.

It is also a useful illustration of the TT's agility. The electronic systems only operate when the car is already beyond normal control, it is chassis ability which still counts, making the TT a competent and rewarding car to drive. As the senior instructor points out: 'ESP will not make the car faster around the track, since it only works once the driver has lost control'. Of course, its function is to help the driver to keep the car on the track after losing control.

The fast lane change exercise carried out with the ESP switched off and the driver not allowed to touch either brake or accelerator, once the TT is up to 50mph or so, is proof enough. The initial avoidance turn is easy enough, the counter-swing large and the need to apply corrective steering quickly is of paramount importance. With ESP active, it's like a second invisible driver has reacted a split second before you, and the system undoubtedly works just as well with the skilled driver as it does to assist the less experienced. Overall the safety is stressed, since none of these systems can make a wet road become dry, reduce that excessive speed on approach to a corner, or defy the laws of physics. However, the way in which the car's systems cope is very impressive.

The next level

It is the stepped structure of the Audi Driving Experience which sets it apart from other manufacturers' driving courses. By using the first day as the entry ticket to the higher echelons of training Audi has taken a leaf out of the books of good racing driver schools. The consequences of attempting to lap the

TTs with DSG transmission and steering wheel shifters make track life easier. (Spectrum Media)

Snow problem: you can take a TT to the limits on the advanced courses. (Audi Driving Experience)

Nürburgring at speed without the fundamentals being in place doesn't bear thinking about. The final exercise on the one-day event at Silverstone was the high speed lapping. Once more this is about discovering and pushing your own limits. There is no instructor in the car. He is in the lead and communicates to all cars via an open radio link. The cars change position in the 'convoy' at regular intervals, and you learn the most at each end. Immediately behind the instructor's leading car you can drive exactly in his wheel tracks, particularly true on the day the author took the course as it rained heavily at Silverstone from first light until evening. As the places are switched you later find yourself at the back of the pack. Slowing to let other cars through naturally leaves you trying to catch up. Your fellow participants immediately ahead will seldom be on the right line, you must find that yourself, and the limits of grip as you attempt to catch up. Preparation indeed for that

Nürburgring adventure, and a fitting climax to a day from which any Audi TT driver, no matter what their experience, will take away a great deal.

For the author, an incredible coincidence marked out the day as being particularly special. At lunch, the table was shared with one of the instructors, a man not usually on the team but who had been brought in for this particular event. Introduced as 'Freddy' it transpired he had once – and only once – contested the Paris–Dakar Rally, and on that one occasion – in 1980 – he won the event. Then, the sudden realisation hit home. This was Freddy Kottulinsky, driver of the Audi-powered VW Iltis, a team of which were entered into the Paris–Dakar to prove the durability of the running gear for use in Audi's then-prototype four-wheel-drive coupé; the quattro.

What are the odds, in the final week of writing this book, to sit at lunch, with the man who had driven to victory the vehicle which was the granddaddy of the whole quattro family? That was an experience which hadn't appeared on the timetable!

Chapter Five

Driving the TT

The emotional aspects involved, often make it difficult to quantify a car's appeal and popularity. With a sports car this situation is even more complex as design seldom lends itself to compromise. Sports cars which lean to the traditions of the breed with racing car values are rarely suitable as every day road cars. They have small cabins, stiff suspension promoting a hard ride, little in the way of stowage space and few of the comforts that are standard on most family cars, such as air-conditioning, in a bid to save weight. At the other end of the scale there are those models which purport to be sports cars but are in fact, merely luxury

convertibles. They offer all manner of creature comforts, with luxuriously appointed cabins, good stowage space, a comfortable ride, large eight or 12-cylinder engines and usually, automatic transmission. Their sheer size and weight means that they stray far from traditional sports car values. To place them on a race track next to a minimalist four-cylinder lightweight example of the sports car breed, serves only to highlight their 'boulevard' credentials.

The Audi TT could be neither of these cars. From its earliest design it had to appeal to those who wished to drive hard over demanding roads, but demanded

Opposite: Twin pipes, black mesh, it's a V6. (Audi Press)

The practicality of the TT is central to its success. (Audi Tradition)

Compact but powerful, sums up the TT, particularly this 3.2-litre car. (Audi UK)

comfort on city streets. It had to offer stowage space for practical daily use and reasonable fuel consumption for a decent touring range. Above all, it had to feel like a sports car to drivers who had no desire to give up the comforts, ease of driving and sheer civility they had grown to expect from driving performance hatchbacks and saloons. Not withstanding its designer's comments that people would want to 'wear' the TT in addition to driving it, it had to appeal to those with no enthusiasm for driving, but a desire to own a good-looking car. A wide design brief if ever there was one.

On several levels

Such a wide design brief can only be applied to a range of models, not just one single design. From the very early days of the TT's design work it was envisaged that the car would be offered with a range of engine outputs and be available with both front and four-wheel drive. The number of drive wheels would be packaged with the power of the engine so that it would not be possible to have the more powerful engine with only front-wheel drive, or the least powerful engine in quattro form. This would give the TT a starting point – and price – comparable with that of the smaller traditional roadsters.

Although it was several years into the TT's life before a six-cylinder car appeared, the earliest of Freeman Thomas's design sketches had a note of a VR6-powered A3C – the TT's project name. Audi never used the VR6 engine as such – it powered the high-performance versions of VW's Golf and the Golf-based Corrado – but the 3.2-litre V6 engine, a narrow-angle design, effectively – and somewhat belatedly – replaced the VR6 in the flagship VW Golf, the R32.

The reason that the narrow-angle V6 lends itself so well to the TT is that it can be housed in the wide but

DID YOU KNOW?

The original designs for the A3C noted a 200PS maximum output and the three power outputs of the 1.8T engine, 150PS, 180PS and 225PS, are created mainly by differences in the intercooling. The 20-valve quattro had four valves in each of its five cylinders. The TT's engines are 20-valve, with five valves in four cylinders.

shallow engine compartment, designed for a transversely mounted engine and transaxle unit. Without this design of engine, it is doubtful that the TT would ever have used a six-cylinder engine and it is all the more understandable why Audi developed three outputs for the highly advanced 1.8T engine. With standard turbocharging and two levels of intercooling this four-cylinder unit develops 150PS, 180PS or 225PS. The use of the same basic engine in three states of tune shows the flexibility that turbocharger technology can bestow upon a single engine concept. It has another effect in that it gives three different characters to the car.

The 150PS engine offers the most flexibility for town driving, the least change in character as the turbo boost takes hold – simply as it has the lowest level of boost of the trio – and with only front-wheel drive it makes for the most familiar handling balance for those drivers not used to a full-blown sports car.

The level of flexibility is brought about by the excellent 'breathing' of the five-valves-per-cylinder design. Although the engine does not develop its full 150PS until 5,700rpm the torque of 210Nm (155lb ft) is available all the way from 1,750rpm to 4,600rpm. This

For many people, the Roadster is the true embodiment of the sports car genre. (What Car?**)**

means the 150PS engine needs only a five-speed transmission since the reduction in driving torque after the next higher gear is selected, is minimal.

Starter motor

The 150PS car serves as the TT's entry-level model. Its price and performance are aimed at the first-time sports car buyer or maybe those who 'wear' the car more than drive it. After all, you get the same styling and build quality in all TTs so the 150PS car is far from being a poor substitute.

For many people too, the Roadster is the true embodiment of the sports car genre and for these drivers the Coupé is a little too mature, perhaps too sensible. Certainly, if you want to turn heads as you drive along, the TT Roadster is the car to achieve it.

The sports car values of the TT begin with first impressions. You drop down into the driver's seat and immediately feel that calling this car the A3 Coupé would have been a terrible oversight; Roadster says it all. The electric window which twitched down a fraction as you opened the door, nips back into its seal on the underside of the soft-top upon closing it. Immediately the TT feels alive.

The driving position is sporting, but not compromised. Headroom and legroom are ample, the seat support is good and the leather 'pads' on the side of the

Above: The driving position is sporting, but comfortable. This is a V6 car with DSG transmission. (Audi UK)

Right: By careful positioning of the switches the interior looks more traditional. (Spectrum Media)

centre console's aluminium struts are not merely for show; along with the foot rest to the left of the clutch pedal they are your brace on right-hand corners. It might not say quattro on the rear of this TT, but it can still grip the road where others might not.

Those padded struts tell the whole story of the TT's interior – and indeed its whole persona – in a nutshell. The TT has to feel like a sports car and behave like a sports car but with none of the traditional sports car compromises, discomforts or idiosyncrasies. The TT Roadster in 150PS form is where this compromise is most vivid.

To keep the interior looking sporting – even sparse – the design team have hidden away most of the electronic controls. The release for the fuel filler, the boot lid and the switch to isolate the interior sensor for the alarm, are covered by a sliding panel forward of the

gear lever. It looks like the top of the transmission tunnel in a traditional rear-drive roadster and mimics the shape and line of the 'trunking' for the facia vents in the top of the dashboard.

The electric window switches are tucked away behind the door pull/armrest in each door, while the control for the electric mirrors nestles next to the armrest in the driver's door. The switches for the electric folding soft-top are discretely positioned aft of the hand brake.

The apparent lack of numerous electric systems

makes the TT Roadster's interior seem all the more traditional, and uncluttered. Designs using the heads of small bolts to finish the steering wheel centre, gear lever and even facia vents adds to the effect of bare aluminium. It has an 'engineered' look to the interior. The TT looks and feels, in a tactile manner, like a traditional sports racing car, but offers the creature comforts of modern motoring. That's the sort of compromise we don't mind accepting in our cars. The 150PS Roadster is far from compromised on the road however. The engine is particularly characterful, for what in essence is the entry-level car. The flexibility from low engine speeds is superb and Audi has given it a fair amount of whistle from the turbo, particularly as you lift from the throttle to change gear. Combined with the low-mounted seating position, direct and weighty steering and quick gearchange, the 'TT for everyone' feels every inch the sports car. Lower the roof and the effect is amplified. Then the exhaust note curls up over the boot lid and the turbo's effect upon the exhaust tone is obvious.

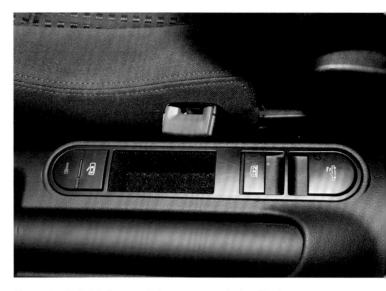

The roof and wind deflector switches are next to the hand brake.
(Spectrum Media)

With the roof down, the open road is the place for the 150PS Roadster.
(Spectrum Media)

Above: The wind deflector is a welcome asset on colder days. Its curved glass profile follows the TT's roll hoops. (Spectrum Media)

Right: The design and effect of the wind deflector is shown here. (Audi Tradition)

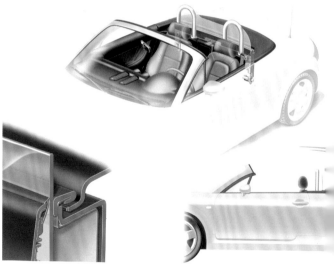

The roof is supremely easy to operate. In the centre, above the windscreen, a handle like that of a briefcase is unfolded from its locked position and turned, releasing two 'claws' which latch into the top of the windscreen frame.

The roof instantly springs clear of the windscreen and the side windows twitch down a little to create some clearance from the roof seals.

Once this is done all that is needed is to press and hold down the rear end of the roof switch on the centre panel behind the hand brake and after a few seconds the TT Roadster is an open car. Lift the edge of the wind-deflector switch, adjacent to the roof switch and the profiled glass wind deflector rises into place.

The soft-top cover is housed in the boot and not only keeps dust out of the top but makes the whole thing look a lot neater. Then the open road beckons.

On the road

The TT Roadster like other soft-top cars, is less rigid than the fixed-roof car. This is commonplace since the car's roof supplies a great deal of its rigidity and removing it from the structure can lead to less rewarding handling. It's true that the TT Roadster does display what is commonly called scuttle-shake. This is where, over bumpy roads, a car flexes slightly and becomes obvious when the view of the edge of the rear window, or roll-over bar can be seen to move slightly in relation to the rear-view mirror itself, which is on the windscreen. This is quite normal, but the TT displays little in the way of reduced road holding or handling balance as a result. Audi's engineers worked hard on this area of the TT Roadster, knowing that the open car

This is the extent to which Audi's engineers went to make the Roadster rigid. (Audi Tradition)

was likely to prove just as popular and be endowed with just as much power as the Coupé version.

Being front-wheel drive separates the handling character of the 150 Roadster from the rest of the TT range. Audi has plenty of experience on front-wheel drive and although the quattro really put the latter-day Audis on the map, there are far more front-wheel drive cars made than quattros. Only the TT reverses that balance, as most are only available as quattros.

Obviously, if you press-on hard enough to overcome the grip of the tyres the TT 150 Roadster will understeer, but on a dry road, with this level of power it really only occurs in first and second gears. In wet conditions, naturally grip is lost sooner, but the traction control is noteworthy not for how quickly or strongly it responds, but how delicately it does. Early electronic traction controls were too severe and the driver felt as if the engine had been shut off in mid-corner. The TT 150 Roadster's system allows some wheelspin in the interests of a more natural cornering line and behaviour. It gently applies the brakes to counter the wheelspin but only intervenes seriously if the driver

persists in pressing the throttle to the floor in unsuitable conditions. Driven hard by an experienced and enthusiastic driver, the front-wheel-drive car is no less fun to drive than the quattro versions. This is not always true of front-drive Audis, compared with their more sophisticated sister models.

Naturally, traction out of slow corners is not as good as with the quattro versions, but the front-wheel-drive TT has the same handling balance, correctly weighted and geared steering and the crisp turn-in of the other TTs.

Overall performance is acceptable for the class rather than being extraordinary. The turbo boost is delivered with virtually no lag and in the middle of its rev-range the 150PS engine is a real pleasure to drive. Acceleration obviously cannot match the more powerful cars, but the wide spread of torque means it is easy to drive around in city traffic and still has sufficient urge for safe overtaking on fast roads. Refinement can often be a downside to the soft-top configuration.

The most noticeable aspect of the TT Roadster from this point of view is the exterior noise. Compared with the Coupé, the occupants of the Roadster can more clearly hear other traffic and external sources of noise. At motorway speeds too, the noise level is a little higher,

This 150PS Roadster is front-wheel drive and displays gentle understeer when cornering hard. Note the 'FWD' (front-wheel drive?) numberplate! (*What Car?*)

mainly from the different properties of the soft-top in the airflow, but it is impressively free of rippling or flapping even at high speeds. The level of compromise the driver of a TT Roadster must make is minimal and add the versatility and the sheer physical pleasure of driving an open sports car down a winding country road in the summer, and it is easy to see the Roadster's appeal. This is real sports car experience for a reasonable cost and in terms of the amount of fun compared with the amount spent, the TT 150 Roadster is impressive.

Close relations

The 180PS version is often considered the best-kept secret of the TT family – particularly those with the six-speed gearbox.

The 180PS engine has a 9.5:1 compression ratio and develops its 180PS output at 5,500 rpm with its maximum torque of 235Nm (173lb ft) from 1,950rpm through to 5,000rpm. This gives flexibility equal to the 150PS engine, albeit shifted as a whole slightly towards the higher end of the rev range. Even so, the 'torque plateau' – achieved by the sophisticated breathing of the engine, through the five-valve layout and the small KKK model K03 turbocharger means the 180PS is just as

docile around town. With the six-speed transmission – earlier cars had five speeds – it offers excellent all-round ability from city traffic to demanding mountain roads. The relatively small turbo picks up speed rapidly for high boost pressures at low engine speeds, and incorporates an air divert valve when the engine is on overrun. This reduces the slowing of the turbo and hence throttle response is improved, minimising 'turbo-lag'.

The 225PS engine although sharing the basic design of the 150/180PS units has a lower compression ratio at 9.0:1 in place of the other engines' 9.5:1. This lowering of the so-called 'static' compression ratio is common practice in higher boost engines. This more powerful unit uses the slightly larger KKK turbo, the K04, and its boost pressure can reach up to 2 bar. Increasing the boost is only part of the answer and to maintain the flexibility required, the higher output engine has not one intercooler – as in the 180PS unit – but two. In addition, the exhaust and inlet manifolds are different, the air cleaner is larger and the internal components of piston and connecting rods are stronger, with a different dual-mass flywheel and uprated clutch completing the differences between the two engines.

The engine takes on a slightly higher revving character. The maximum output of 225PS is generated at 5,900rpm while the peak torque, albeit still spread over a wide plateau, is higher in the rev range. Some 280Nm (206lb ft) is generated from 2,200rpm to 5,500rpm.

The 180PS and 225PS models formed the entire range of the TT initially, and were separated by their gearboxes and overall performance. The 180PS was launched with a five-speed manual transmission while the 225PS had a six-speed unit. This not only created a difference in the performance of the two cars, but was, in part, a requirement of the 225PS engine's slightly higher revving nature. The 180PS unit was somewhat more flexible. The arrival of the 150PS front-wheel-drive Roadster challenged the 180PS car's position, to some

extent, as the entry-level model. Giving it a six-speed gearbox increased its performance and gave the TT range a further step in the performance scale, in expectation of the arrival of the 250PS V6 engine.

Driving the 180PS in five-speed form immediately gives you the impression of that flexibility. It feels very much like the 150PS engine the way it will lug from low revs but keep on pulling right around the tachometer. Traction is simply superb. As this is the least powerful of the quattro cars it is incredibly difficult to break its hold on the tarmac. In dry conditions the TT 180 quattro is as near a foolproof sports car as it's possible to get. The Haldex-coupling system naturally has a bias to the front wheels, since it is only when these begin to outpace the rear wheels that the four-wheel drive really comes into effect. Pushing the car hard around second and third gear corners on the test track you can gradually develop the same gently understeering stance that the 150PS car adopts, but you are travelling a good deal quicker at the time. Out of really tight corners excessive use of the throttle will bring in the traction control system on the inside front wheel, despite the quattro system's best

The four-cylinder turbocharged quattro TT models share the same handling characteristics. (*What Car?*)

efforts to handle the applied torque, but it is supremely controllable for all that.

Sure, with such a high degree of grip and cornering force, lifting from the accelerator in mid-bend will bring about a change in character, particularly if revving hard in an intermediate gear at the time. The TT however displays only moderate oversteer and only by driving with the ESP switched off – again on the test track – can you ever provoke full oversteer. It is easy to catch on the quick steering too, and at this point it feels very much like the on-limit behaviour of the original Ur quattro.

Drive a 180PS TT with the six-speed gearbox and although its dynamics are identical to the five-speed car, the flow of acceleration is more linear. The additional ratio, acting upon that flat torque curve means that although the car feels less punchy in each gear, the overall performance is impressive. Six-speed gearboxes are often used to mask a steep drop-off in the engine's torque characteristics, but the 180PS engine is very well mannered from this point of view so the result is the feeling of a close-ratio competition car. For drivers who choose their sports car for its involvement rather than outright power the TT quattro 180, has few rivals.

If the TT 180 has a handling balance reminiscent of the Ur quattro, then surely there is something more emotive about the TT Coupé 225PS car. A 20-valve turbo-charged quattro four-wheel-drive coupé boasting around 220bhp and acceleration from rest to 100kph (62mph) in around seven seconds. Sounds familiar? Then surely this is the spiritual successor to the legendary 20-valve Ur quattro. The A4 might have the same level of interior

The modern TT is faster in all areas compared with the legendary quattro. (Audi UK)

A TT and a winding road. All the enthusiast needs. (Audi UK)

accommodation, but it's a saloon, so for quattro fanatics it has to be a quattro Coupé which takes on the mantle.

In truth, the TT 225 is faster both in a straight line and around corners than the legendary car, but it has 20 years of suspension and tyre progress to thank, not to mention more favourable weight distribution.

The TT 225, for so long the flagship of the TT range is deserving of the reverence bestowed upon it by fans of the range and of sporting cars in general. Early design sketches of the TT even showed it in a mock-up rally car guise, sporting the red and white Audi works colours of the 1980s rally cars. If Audi had continued in rallying then surely the TT quattro 225 would have formed the basis for the attack. Once tuned, its engine would easily be capable of the required 300bhp and its all-electronic four-wheel-drive system is perfectly suited to the differential and torque bias controls of latter-day WRC cars.

Right: A 3.2V6 in Germany. (Audi UK)

Below: The TT 3.2-litre V6 makes for refined high-speed cruising. (*What Car?*)

The daydream can become reality on any old stretch of winding country road. Where geography is the limit to top speed and not the law, the TT 225 can be driven hard, safe in the knowledge that forward vision and the approaching corner will keep the car within the confines of the road. There are those who would have you believe that four-wheel drive, the grip of modern tyres and all the electronic traction aids will detract from a sports car experience. It is quite the opposite. Compared with a classic car which slides around at lowly speed, engaging its driver in car control at safe velocities, the TT may indeed make it look all too easy, but the sensations of acceleration, braking and cornering that it can apply would be difficult to achieve in many a serious competition car only a few years ago.

The TT 225 quattro is one of those cars which is more

The DSG transmission is happy in town or on the open road. (*What Car?*)

impressive after a drive. When you can sit down and reflect upon the grip, the acceleration and the sheer ease with which it covers a winding road you realise it is a car that works with you, and helps you, and is no less rewarding than one which you have to master, wrestle and coax to do as you wish. Many sports cars fall into the latter group. The TT 225 quattro is definitely one of the former.

The outright power of the TT 225 quattro is not its greatest asset, although the surge from low revs to full turbo-boost is impressive in itself. It is the fact that with so much power the four-wheel-drive system is

DID YOU KNOW?

The 3.2V6 is effectively half a W12 engine which also uses 15° angles between its paired cylinder banks.

actually tested to some degree, particularly where the road is wet, bumpy or both. It could be argued that with modern electronic traction aids the 180PS car need not be equipped with four-wheel-drive and there may be some truth in that. However, anyone who has driven some of the 200+bhp front-wheel-drive hatchbacks which exist, will be aware of just how little of that power is actually transmitted to the road. At least in the lowest three gears. The electronics intervene to keep the power under control and where the TT quattro will accelerate strongly without recourse to electronic assistance the front-drive cars will either spin the power away or have the engine limited by the traction control system. Right back at the earliest design stages, Audi's engineers pencilled-in the front-drive car at 125PS and 150PS with the quattro at 150PS and 180-200PS. The advances in both tyre technology and electronic traction aids between those early designs and the TT reaching production have not changed the rules. Power is no use if it cannot be transmitted to the road. That was the original

thinking behind the 1980 Audi quattro and it is still as valid today.

Mature thinking

The 3.2-litre V6 engine gives the TT a whole new dimension. It provides the car with a more mature persona, and has the number of cylinders required to compete with the growing band of competitors from Japanese and fellow German manufacturers. Early design sketches for the TT noted its use of the VW VR6 engine, and the 3.2-litre unit, being a narrow, 15° vee engine is its modern embodiment. The advantage of just 25PS over the most powerful of the four-cylinder turbo engines used in the TT may seem of limited benefit, but the gains are real enough. Being naturally aspirated means power delivery is more linear and in many respects smoother than that of the 225PS engine. However, it lacks that surge of power which makes the 225 TTs feel as if they are accelerating even faster than

The TT 3.2V6 quattro corners with gentle understeer, but it's moving quickly just the same! (*What Car?*)

Launch control makes this the most common view that other drivers have of the TT with 3.2V6 and DSG. (*What Car?*)

they really are. The 3.2V6 gives the opposite impression and the car doesn't feel very quick until you glance at the speedometer. The V6 offers a greater level of refinement for long-distance cruising and this is apparent in the way the car travels more quickly than it feels.

The sound the V6 makes is noteworthy too. The exhaust is muted in city driving and motorway cruising, but when the driver hits full throttle and the revs begin to climb the 3.2-litre takes on a full-blooded V6 howl. It is a free-revving engine too, considering its relatively large capacity. At 3.2 litres it is considerably bigger than most V6 units which average 2.5 litres and some Japanese units have been less than 2 litres (122cu in). Although the 225PS engine develops its peak torque at lower revs, the greater overall torque of the V6 shows in the middle of the rev range and the newer TT engine actually has a more 'traditional' feel to its characteristics. For buyers in this sector it also represents a more upmarket engine choice. For many the turbocharged engine is still seen as rather raucous and frantic. In truth, most modern turbo engines have had these characteristics engineered-out, and this is certainly the case with the TT's engines, but often the perception persists.

The 3.2V6 only really comes into its own when paired with DSG transmission. This automatic transmission, originally tested in the fearsome Sport quattro S1 rally car does more than give the TT a smooth operating transmission, it expands and amplifies the car's whole character.

DSG, described earlier in the book, is not a conventional automatic with a fluid coupling but is effectively an automated six-speed manual device. The key to its rapid gear-changing abilities is that unlike similar automated versions of manual gearboxes it does not declutch, select a new gear and then re-engage the drive. It does it all in one action, the gearbox having two clutches, one controlling first, third and fifth gears, the other second, fourth and sixth. This results in a near-instant gear change under full power and the driver never lifts off the accelerator. Impressive in theory; impressive in practice.

Automatic improvement

From the driver's point of view DSG transmission looks and feels like a conventional automatic. The standard selector offers Sport mode and a Tiptronic gate for manual shifts with accompanying steering wheel-mounted paddles. The car even 'creeps' as you release the brakes. However, as it uses friction clutches, it can engage drive slowly and smoothly or more aggressively, just as the driver could with a clutch pedal. In city traffic it's as easy as a conventional automatic, although the

driver has to become accustomed to its characteristics. Plant your foot too firmly on the throttle and the TT will feel jerky. Also, you can catch it out if you are braking gently for a junction and then demand power suddenly, particularly if the transmission needs to downshift. However, it has no greater delay than a conventional automatic downshifting.

In Sport mode, DSG holds on to the gears until the engine hits maximum revs and downshifts at quite high road speeds. It is programmed to always have peak power engine revs operating. As a result, it is probably the only automatic transmission which you could drive around a racetrack and never need to use manual override. Its automatic 'blipping' of the throttle to smooth those high-speed downshifts is reason enough to specify this option.

However, DSG feels best when the steering wheel paddles are used to shift gears manually. Located on the

A German-market V6 DSG with optional wheelstyle. (Audi Press)

back of the steering wheel spokes they are positioned perfectly for operating with first and second fingers on each hand. Left to change down, right to change up. With the shift lever over in Tiptronic mode you can use the lever or the paddles to change gear. If you operate the paddles in 'D' you have manual override. Thirty seconds after using the paddles, the gearbox reverts to full automatic.

Ready for launch

DSG has a very impressive party trick however; launch control. This mimics a racing start executed by the driver with a conventional manual gearbox and clutch, providing maximum acceleration from rest. You bring the TT to a halt, switch off the ESP, select Sport mode with the automatic shift lever and then hold down the brake pedal with your left foot. This sequence sets the system and first gear has been selected with

both clutches open. Normally, if you pressed the accelerator, the clutch would engage and the TT would move off. However in launch control mode this doesn't apply.

Holding the car with your left foot on the brake, you floor the throttle, the system holds the engine at 3,200rpm, and then you release the brake pedal.

A fraction of a second later the system releases the brake and rapidly engages the clutch. Moderate wheelspin accompanies full acceleration and the gearbox shifts up at maximum revs through the gears.

Switching off the ESP allows some wheelspin proving that even in a car with such technology to aid the driver, on all but the most slippery surface, this is still the best way to take off.

Mature the V6 might be, but it still offers a great deal of fun as a driver's car. It's a refined long-distance cruiser and a winding country road burner too – what else do you want from a performance coupé?

The TT's looks always dominate, even when it's parked. (Audi Press)

Choosing and buying a TT

There used to be only two ways to buy a car: new or used. Today, you need not buy the car at all, with various contract or lease agreements available to the private motorist as well as the business buyer. These are not restricted to new cars either, and the various methods of funding the car through finance have made things even more complex.

Buying a new TT

Consider yourself lucky, if you are to embark on the enjoyable, and enviable task of choosing and specifying a new Audi TT. With coupé and roadster body styles, two and four-wheel-drive quattro drivelines, manual and DSG transmission and a massive list of options, you can personalise the car to a high degree. However, it is not merely the options on the car which you have to consider, most likely you will need to consider some form of finance.

We live in a credit-rich world and the car is generally financed by this means in some way or other. Just like the options in sourcing the vehicle in the first place, by dealership, independent supplier, or via direct sales on the Internet, you have the same wide choice in finance methods. If you are buying your TT new, you have a number of finance options.

A new TT is very appealing, but consider your finance options carefully. (Audi UK)

Straightforward finance or hire purchase is the most common method of funding a new private car. If you already have a credit arrangement for your existing car, it can be beneficial to stay with the same finance company for the new one. If not, then shop around for the best deal or use your figures to negotiate a better rate from the dealer.

Buyers generally don't shop around for finance, and having negotiated long and hard on the deal for the new car, can then lose much of that on the financing. Don't let the euphoria of your new TT cloud your judgement, but do the deal for the car first, get the price agreed, and then look at the financial situation.

Research the rate at your own bank, at least one other, and a couple of independents, such as on-line loans. Dealer-supplied finance offering straightforward hire or lease-purchase can be the better option if you intend to keep the vehicle for more than say, three

Choose the wrong finance, and this will not be the only hill you have to climb. (Audi UK)

years. Also, it is an easier option for many people as the security for the finance is the vehicle itself, but you may pay more interest than the best loan rate.

Also consider not only insurance protection for the repayments, so that the finance continues to be paid if you are unable to work for some reason, but also the entirely separate issue of asset protection. This is intended to make up for the difference between the amount you owe to the finance company and the amount paid to you by your insurers should the car be stolen or damaged so badly that it is a total loss or write-off. The market value of the car – even one which holds its value as strongly as the TT – will, in the early stages of the car's life and finance agreement, be less than the total amount including interest still owing on it. This is worth looking into, but calculate it carefully and if you pay a large deposit upfront, such protection may be redundant.

Interest-free finance can seem a very attractive option too, although it is seldom offered on cars like the TT as it is more normally available on high-volume brands whose lifeblood is sales quantity rather than high profit per unit; the operating principle of premium brands like Audi.

The offer of interest-free finance would seem ideal – after all, nobody likes paying interest. However, you will have to put down a big deposit, usually 30 to 50 per cent of the list price. Most interest-free agreements are

over only two years at the most, so even with a large deposit the monthly amounts are still considerable. You might not be paying any interest, but the dealer is. You pay the dealer back by not having any discount on the car and the big initial payment. The old adage of never getting something for nothing, is the finance industry's mission statement.

Why buy?

If you are someone who likes to change their car on a regular basis to keep up with the latest developments, then it might be more beneficial not to buy the car at all. The system of contract hire or straightforward leasing is one widely used for the sourcing of vehicles for business users. From trucks to items of plant and equipment, right through to the company chief executive's limo, all are most likely to be leased in some way, rather than purchased outright.

For the private motorist this is also now an option and the various schemes on the market operate in much the same way as those for the business user. Basically, you are paying for the depreciation of the car, and with a TT that can be less than other sports coupés, so this

route might be more attractive for the Audi buyer than those tempted by other brands. The reason is simple. The more the car is worth at the end of the lease period, normally three years, the less you will pay per month, compared with a car of the same original list price which depreciates more rapidly.

Schemes available offer the driver the option of making a final larger payment at the end of the period to own the vehicle, or to change to a new vehicle using the existing one's value as a deposit, or merely walk away.

Go into such schemes with your eyes open; it's only a finance deal like any other. Obviously, the final value is calculated against the condition and mileage of the vehicle, so if you do regular mileage such schemes can work well, but if your mileage is not easy to predict this might not be the best route. Also, do not be tempted to put too much into the deferred payment. It might seem tempting to put off that big payment for three years, but if it is equal to, instead of less than, the

A higher viewpoint: why buy when you could hire or lease your TT? (Audi UK)

Be realistic with your finances: don't let the wind in your hair go to your head! (*What Car?*)

final value of the vehicle, you then have no money for the deposit on the next vehicle. Such schemes are ideal if you wish to change to a new car every two or three years, if you wish to keep it for longer than that, a standard hire purchase agreement will usually work out cheaper.

The whole scheme hangs on the guaranteed future value of the car, although it goes under many different names. This value, deducted from the purchase price, sets the monthly payments. However, that future value is set to ensure that the finance company doesn't lose. Your TT might be worth considerably more, so a straightforward finance deal to buy the car can work out cheaper, even if you always intended to change it at three years old. If you intend to keep it for longer and would end up paying this future value to take ownership of the car, then you're certainly better off going for a straightforward finance deal in the first place.

Remember that whatever scheme or finance deal you take out, you are merely slicing up the same cake, in different ways. Get all the figures, sit down and calculate your best route. Consider all the ways of insuring or protecting your payments for peace of mind

and above all be realistic about the amount you can afford to pay back each month.

Buying a used TT

The Audi TT differs from many used high-performance coupés on the UK market in that there are few unofficially imported models, which differ from the official UK-specification cars.

Although a huge number of Japanese imports, not officially offered on the market, have found favour in the UK, the TT has always been biased towards the performance end of the range in its biggest export market.

Indeed, it wasn't until July 2003, that Audi offered the 150PS front-wheel-drive TT Roadster for the first time in the UK. Front-wheel-drive Roadsters dating from before this period will be unofficial imports, but this model is not the most popular in any case.

Of course, left-hand-drive versions in the UK will be unofficial imports, although unlike vehicles from other parts of the world, the European specification is broadly similar, particularly so from a mechanical point of view.

It is unlikely, but you might even come across early German-specification cars without the revised suspension and aerodynamic aids. These cars should be avoided, if only from the viewpoint of a poor resale value.

All at sea? Make sure you know the history of a used TT even if it looks perfect. (Audi UK)

Make no mistake, the TT is a sophisticated and complex car. Until the arrival of the 3.2-litre V6 engine and the 150PS Roadster in July 2003, all TTs officially sold in the UK were four-wheel drive and turbocharged. Although drawing heavily on more mundane models in the Audi range, the TT is not merely a coupé-bodied version of a family hatchback, as are some of its competitors – with a simple four-cylinder engine and front-wheel drive. Furthermore, not all are treated with the respect that they deserve. A thorough checking of all the car's major systems is important, particularly if buying from a private seller, where there is no warranty cover should the worst happen. Any Audi TT you consider should have a full service history, preferably with all the invoices to back it up, and a correct mileage pattern over its life too. Be suspicious of TTs with wildly varying mileage across similar periods, the mileage might have been misrepresented, or the car off the road for a long time due to accident damage or other major repair.

Always check that the VIN number and engine number of the car matches that on the registration document, and never buy a TT without the registration document, whatever excuse you are given for the car's current owner not being in possession of it. If it has been lost, or destroyed it is up to the current owner to get a duplicate from the licensing authority.

Check the car's history for any outstanding finance or indeed if it has been stolen, if buying privately. Check out specialist dealers' warranty offers too, and make sure any warranty is worth the paper it's written on.

When going to look at a used TT it can be useful to take a friend with you, especially if you are not the world's most expert car buyer, not only does this give you another pair of eyes, but an unbiased opinion to counter your possibly blinkered enthusiasm for the car. Remember too that there are a lot of TTs on the market, never make a snap decision and even if it seems the best TT in the world, go home and think about it.

DID YOU KNOW?

Without the correct registration documents you have no legal claim on the car, no matter how much you've paid for it. So, check the car's financial history; if you buy a car with finance still outstanding, you will become liable for that amount in addition to your purchase price.

A straight deal

With a high-performance car the first thing to look at is the bodywork. Minor dents or scratches will be obvious, as will their cause, but more serious accidents could spell trouble. Look for over spray – the car's paint colour on areas you would not expect it – on plastic trim, under the wheelarches etc., this will show it's been repaired after a crash, and not very professionally either. It might sound obvious, but if the car is a different colour anywhere, under the trim in the luggage bay, around the inner wings in the engine bay, or beneath the carpets, ask the seller why.

Although the TT is low, try to get a good look at the underside of the car. A torch is useful here. The aerodynamic undertrays are prone to damage particularly if the previous owner has been trying to emulate some boyhood rally hero over the local back roads. Check for scrapes on the lower suspension links too while you're under there and you should look for any fluid leaks.

Stone chips along the nose of the TT will be common with higher mileage cars; this is where you need to look at several examples, since a car purporting to be low mileage with a tatty lived-in look to its bodywork and paint might be telling a different story. Scratching from automatic car washes is common and can be seen easily in strong light. This is normally an indication that the TT was owned by a business user from new, rather than an enthusiast private motorist. When viewing a number of cars it is worth keeping a note of each.

Check the sills for damage, being low means that the TT can scrape on the ground if driven over particularly rough surfaces and also ensure that it has not been jacked-up using the wrong part of the sills, distortion here can spell more trouble than just a replacement panel, and serious distortion can even misalign suspension or driveline components.

Check the alloy wheels for signs of damage. Minor scrapes can be common where the car has touched the kerb, but a serious impact can misalign the steering or even suspension components. Just one obviously new alloy wheel on the car might indicate such an incident.

Look at the tyres. Uneven wear across the width of the front ones indicates misalignment of the steering, but look at the rear tyres too as they may have been swapped around with the front ones to hide the problem. Check also that they are the correct tyres for

The door sills and their trim plates will show up signs of hard use. (Spectrum Media)

the car. TTs should have at least a 'W' speed-rated tyre, if not, it's a sure sign that the owner is skimping on maintenance. If the tyres have different wear rates from left to right or front to rear the owner has replaced them in ones and twos, another economy measure which could also affect the car's stability in an emergency. Furthermore, if you buy the car and run it with the incorrect speed-rated tyres, your insurance might be void in the event of an accident. If the owner has cut corners on maintenance here, what else might be wrong, that you cannot see?

Pay particular attention to the soft-top on Roadster models as damage here can be expensive to repair – at least a repair that is not visible from a mile away – and naturally any damage which leads to water ingress to the interior will just add to your troubles. Make sure the protective cover which fits over the top in its folded position is with the car and is in good condition.

Inside story

The interior can provide just as many clues to the car's life, as the exterior can. Obvious signs of high mileage are a scuffed driver's seat and door sill area, worn pedals, or suspiciously new pedals. However, you should also bear in mind that many TT owners will fit after-market adornments, so non-geniune pedals or non-standard kick plates on the sills are not necessarily the evils they might first appear to be.

Check also for signs of damage to the interior. Virtually everything in here is unique to the TT: there is no such thing as a cheap repair to scratched or permanently marked leather or facia trim, the same goes for all the aluminium. Check also for a bad fit in the interior. Like all Audis of its generation, the TT's quality of fit is first rate, a badly fitted facia means its been removed and replaced poorly, another pointer to an accident repair.

It is the mechanical condition of the car which should be your next concern. Most TTs you will find on the used market will be turbocharged as it wasn't until July 2003 that the V6 appeared, so correct servicing is of great importance. Naturally, a full Audi service history is essential but also take note of how well the current owner is looking after the car. Check that the engine bay is clean and ensure there are no oil leaks around the engine and gearbox – there is no such thing as a minor oil leak on a high-revving turbocharged engine such as this. Check the colour of the oil on the dipstick too; it should be golden and

Above: Check alloy wheels for signs of damage. (Spectrum Media)

Below: Look at the interior for signs of heavy wear or bad repair. (Spectrum Media)

Above: Check all the upholstery for clues to the car's history and mileage. Above right: Look at the door trim for signs of repair or for water damage in the Roadster. Below: Access to the rear is tight, and the front seats can become scuffed because of it. (Spectrum Media)

Check the oil level and condition. If it's poor, the rest of the car will be too. Leave it alone. (Spectrum Media)

quite thin if it's the correct high-grade synthetic type. If it's dark coloured or sludge-like put the dipstick back, smile at the current owner politely, and walk away! Check also that the dipstick is showing the correct amount of oil. With long service intervals the responsible owner will check and top-up the oil. If the level is low, leave this TT well alone. The other worthwhile check is for oil emulsification in the oil filler cap after the engine has been run. This shows itself as a frothy white deposit and shows that the oil and coolant have been mixing, a sure sign of cylinder head gasket trouble. Also see if a genuine Audi oil filter is fitted. An Audi dealer would never fit a pattern filter and even an independent garage should fit the genuine part. Anything else and you can take it that the owner has been cutting corners on maintenance.

While on the subject of coolant, check it, and all other fluid levels in the engine bay, just to get a feeling about whether this TT has been properly cared for, or not. The other major component with fluid in it, is at the other end of the car. The Haldex coupling is the heart of the TT quattro's four-wheel-drive system. Do not think of it in the same terms as the axle on an old rear-wheel-drive car, where a bit of oil weeping out is of no major concern. Fluid leaking from the coupling is

bad news and will create serious malfunction of the unit, it could indicate that the coupling has suffered physical damage also, but in any case, it is cause for great concern.

The real test

The turbocharged engine will be the major concern for most buyers of a used TT. Although modern turbocharged petrol units don't deserve the reputation founded by such engines of old, for spectacular failure and a limited service life, you should still check it over carefully. The key to turbo longevity is in how well it has been looked after on a daily basis. This is just as important as correct servicing. The turbocharger unit itself not only runs at very high temperatures but very high revolutions too. At full boost, which may occur from as little as 2,000rpm of engine speed, the turbocharger will be spinning at up to 110,000rpm. To achieve this it has very little mass and inertia, so it spins up rapidly and keeps spinning easily. The problems come when the engine is switched off. From high load, a turbocharged engine should be run at idle for as long as two minutes, to allow the turbo to run down and for its oil supply to continue to flow, helping it to cool. Switch off the engine immediately after hard use and the turbo can still be turning with no oil flow. Not good for its longevity by any means.

Check for signs of turbo troubles on the test drive. If the car smokes as you pull away after a brief halt – at a junction or traffic lights – then it could be leaking oil past the turbocharger seals. This would point to a turbocharger rebuild or replacement which is not cheap. If the engine has been run hard from a cold start the valve guides may have excessive wear, showing the same smoking symptom as oil finding its way into the cylinders. Smoke when accelerating, after a long deceleration – as when descending a long hill – might even point to worn piston rings, resulting in an expensive engine rebuild. All these symptoms are signs that the TT's current or previous owner has failed to understand the character of a high-performance engine and has failed to look after the car properly. You must ask yourself what other areas of the car might have suffered from a similar level of neglect.

Noise from the turbo, in the form of a faint whistle, is

nothing of concern as this is merely the sound of the changes in pressure of the air being fed into the engine. Anything more 'metallic' sounding, or a loud whine should be treated with more concern as this too could point to the effects of oil starvation in the turbocharger. The engine generally should have no unusual characteristics. It should idle smoothly and should pull away cleanly too. The level of electronic control in the Audi engines means that any hesitation or jerkiness in response to smooth accelerator operation by the driver would point to problems in the engine management or physical defects in the inlet or exhaust tracts. In any case, it will not be a simple fix.

The clutch should 'bite' or take up drive from below the halfway point on the pedal travel. A high-mileage car with the clutch bite point high up on the pedal travel would indicate a replacement clutch is around the corner. If the car is otherwise sound this is no real problem, but contact an official Audi centre and get a price before starting negotiations with the seller.

The gearchange should be positive. The gearlever has a relatively 'notchy' feel compared with a family car but all the gears should engage cleanly and quietly. A whine or graunching when changing down could indicate worn synchromesh and a costly gearbox rebuild.

Try to give the car a reasonably long test drive. (Audi UK)

Above: This is a 180PS car as it has a single tailpipe and a quattro badge. Without the quattro badge this would indicate a 150PS front-wheel-drive car. (*What Car?*)

Below: Twin tailpipes indicate this is a 225PS car. The V6 also has twin tailpipes but different aerodynamics and the badge denotes the six-cylinder engine. (*What Car?*)

Left: Check the transmission for trouble, either the manual, or the automatic, as shown here. (Audi UK)

Above: Make sure all the systems on the car work correctly – some are expensive to fix. (Spectrum Media)

Below: Look in every corner for signs of bad repair. (Spectrum Media)

Try to test for the car jumping out of gear when you abruptly decelerate. If it does, cross this one off your list.

The four-wheel-drive quattro running gear gives no indication of its presence. Drivers with a high level of mechanical 'feel' can just detect the transfer of drive to the rear wheels in a TT quattro, particularly when pulling away rapidly on a wet road, but any clanks or bangs are no part of a healthy TT.

The quattro four-wheel-drive system also includes a great deal of electronic control. Ensure that the ABS light illuminates when the ignition is on, but goes out just after the engine has started, if not, there is a problem with the ABS or traction control systems. Make sure the car brakes cleanly and in a straight line. Other than a natural tendency for the wide, low-profile tyres to follow patchy tarmac where pipes or cables have been laid in the road, it should behave impeccably under even the heaviest braking. Always ensure the road is clear behind you for a good distance if you intend to fully test the TT's brakes. Test the climate control with the engine idling at the end of the test drive, unless it is obviously working fine during the drive. Turn the climate control to its coldest setting in 'Auto' and increase the fan speed by a step or two. As the air-conditioning pump engages the engine revs will change slightly under the load and you might even hear a faint knock as the air-conditioner's clutch engages; all this is normal. The air from the facia vents should become very cold within 10 to 20 seconds,

depending upon the temperature of the ambient air. On a very hot day this might take a little longer.

Over and above all these particular checks, use common sense. Never check over a car in fading light, and if it is wet you will not get a true picture of the quality of the paint condition.

If you are buying the car from a private individual meet at their home. A public car park or similar venue would indicate something suspicious such as the car being stolen, or having some other dark side to its past. Never accept any excuse for the lack of a registration document, the owner is the only one with the means to source that document, so if the seller cannot produce it, for whatever colourful reason, walk away.

Get the car checked out professionally too. Not just its physical condition, but its history. HPI the finance register, or motoring organisations such as the RAC or AA Data Check can tell you if the car is stolen, has outstanding finance still owed on it, has been falsely registered or if it has previously been registered as a total loss (write-off) by an insurance company. If it does not check out 100 per cent, call a cab, it will be a small price to pay by comparison!

The TT is a very popular car, and the choice of used models is huge, so there is no need to take any risks when buying a TT.

Also look closely at the paint and panel condition, as well as the interior trim. (Spectrum Media)

Don't go and see a car in the middle of nowhere; arrange to meet at the vendor's address. (Audi UK)

Chapter Seven

Owning and running a TT

Although Audi's TT Coupé and Roadster models are sophisticated and complex pieces of engineering apart from the Haldex coupling at the heart of the TT quattro's four-wheel-drive system, most of the major components are proven elsewhere within the Audi or VW ranges.

For the enthusiast owner, the TT should not be a difficult car to care for, and neither should it require any real expert knowledge or techniques. Gone are the days when sports car owners had to be part racing driver, part mechanic and part oil tycoon. However, the TT is not a car which can be neglected. Simple, regular checks and maintenance are all that the owner needs to do between scheduled services, to keep the car in top condition.

Simple and regular maintenance will keep your TT looking as good as new. (Audi UK)

Long service

The TT, like other Audis of its generation is designed to take advantage of variable service intervals. This is one of the areas in which electronic engine management has totally changed the modern car. Instead of having fixed intervals for its services, such as every year or 12,000 miles, the TT informs the owner when it needs to be serviced. With fixed intervals some cars would be serviced earlier than they needed to be, but those which undergo heavy use, a lot of stop-start traffic driving, or are used to the absolute maximum on club racetrack days, would be serviced less than required. The variable servicing system takes account of this. The system measures a huge amount of data, the number of cold starts in a given period, how hard the car is driven, all are used to calculate its optimum service schedule. The maximum period the system will allow is two years or 19,000 miles between services. This is the 'best case'

Above: Check the oil regularly. Long service intervals mean the workshop sees your TT infrequently. Below: Always have at least this much of the correct oil to hand. You might need to top up, particularly in the early stages of a new car's life. (Both Spectrum Media)

scenario, if the car has a more arduous daily routine, the period will be less.

Such extended service periods are not without their problems however, and some owners and business users of such cars tend to forget that interim checks are all the more important when the workshop sees the car less frequently than used to be the case. On the TT it is important to check the major levels regularly, particularly the engine oil.

A good rule of thumb is to check the engine oil as often as you fill the car with fuel, or many owners get into the habit of checking it once per week. The high-performance engines in the TT will be seriously damaged by being run with insufficient oil. Regular

While you have the bonnet up, check all the other levels too. This is the windscreen washer tank on a 150PS car. (Spectrum Media)

checking also gives an early indication of any problems and the workshop technicians will appreciate as much information as possible on how much oil the car might be using, or losing, in the event of a fault.

Check coolant, power steering, and brake fluid levels too and ensure all are correct. The brake fluid level will drop very slightly over several thousand miles as the brake pads wear and the self-adjust mechanism accounts for this, moving the pads slightly closer to the discs and allowing a small, additional amount of fluid into the system from the reservoir. However, it is such a gradual process that it is difficult to see the change in level. If the brake fluid level drops suddenly, then get the system checked as there is obviously a leak somewhere and the car should not be driven until it has been found and rectified. The best option might be to have the car transported to the workshop, as your breakdown and recovery cover will allow for this in such a situation, as the car may not be roadworthy.

Always check the oil and coolant levels after the car has stood for several minutes with the engine switched off. Ideally, only check the coolant level when the engine is cold to avoid heat expansion giving a false level. Only the correct coolant mix should be used and

Competing in the German Touring Car series, this TT has its own team of technicians. (Audi Press)

the engine oil must be of the grade recommended by Audi. This will be shown in the handbook for each particular engine and operating environment. All are high-grade synthetic oils, so ensure you have at least a one-litre bottle of the correct oil at all times, for topping up.

The turbocharger places greater emphasis on the engine oil than a naturally aspirated engine would. The oil is responsible for cooling the turbo and this places greater loads on the oil itself, making interim checks and correct servicing of paramount importance. While under the bonnet don't forget the windscreen washer level and have a general look around to check that nothing is loose, no pipes or hoses are damaged and no wiring is out of its clips, potentially coming into contact with hot or rotating components. Check the

condition of the drive belts for the power steering pump and alternator too, and that the thermostatically controlled electric cooling fan spins freely at the touch of one finger.

Driving at 110,000rpm

Care of the TT's engine is not just about lifting the bonnet however. The care of any high-performance engine, and particularly a turbocharged one, is down to how it is driven.

The fundamental thing to understand is that the turbo's rotation is not physically linked to the engine. Since only the exhaust gas flow and pressure drive the turbocharger, it revolves at a different speed from the engine, accelerates and decelerates at a different rate from the engine, and even continues to turn when the engine has stopped. This latter factor is the most critical, since when the engine stops, so does the flow of oil.

It should go without saying that you should never drive an engine hard from cold. Never start it up and rev it any more than the minimum speed you need to make the car pull away and if possible, let the engine idle for a few seconds before driving off whether hot or cold. The same rules apply to the turbo. Do not load the engine by flooring the accelerator at low engine speed while cold as this will bring the turbocharger up to full speed. Shifting up the gearbox at very low revs and making the engine work, is just as bad as revving it hard from a start.

Allow the engine to reach full operating temperature before you demand high performance from it. The TT generally has such reserves of performance and such a power-to-weight ratio that you need not demand much from it at all, to maintain the speed of the surrounding traffic.

Although sports cars of old needed to be run hard – merely commuting around the city was the worst thing you could do with a performance engine – the Audi TT's units are not so temperamental and it can be used as a daily commuting car with no detriment to its overall performance. The only downside is that you will find the variable service indicator will appear more

frequently. However, the TT is designed for driving, and a correctly maintained engine will not suffer from being driven to extract its full performance, the owner merely needs to understand the difference between using and abusing the car.

This is most critical when it comes to stopping a turbocharged engine. Since the turbo spins independently of the engine – at up to 110,000 rpm – if you drive a turbocharged TT hard and then switch off the engine immediately after the car comes to a halt, you can cause serious damage to the bearings and seals in the turbocharger. This is because the oil flow stops when the engine does, but the turbo might still be spinning. Always allow the engine to idle for at least 30 seconds, and if using the car hard

Under pressure. Tyres are the most important parts of the quattro driveline. (Spectrum Media)

over winding or mountainous roads, idle the engine for up to two minutes. This allows the turbocharger to come to rest with oil flowing around it and once the turbo has run down it allows the flow of oil to cool it. The turbocharger itself will radiate a lot of heat into the engine bay, so the best scenario is for the car to be driven more sedately after a hard drive before allowing reasonable idle period and then switching off. On most journeys this is automatically the case. Seldom do you reach your destination immediately after very hard use of the engine, but for those owners who use their TT on racetrack days, always drive a slower cooling-down lap, or allow at least two minutes of idling, before shutting off the engine.

Making contact

The TT might have one of the most sophisticated four-wheel-drive and electronic traction control systems on

Always remove stones which are stuck in the tread. (Spectrum Media)

The directional tyre has a sidewall marking to indicate its intended rotation. Do not run it backwards. (Spectrum Media)

the market, but it relies on four very traditional components for its success.

Check the tyre pressures regularly, once a week on a high-mileage car, and at worst each time the car is washed, for instance. Always check the pressures when cold, this is the condition in which the handbook lists the pressures. However, the enthusiast might also make a note of the hot pressures. This allows a roadside check of the tyres if any problem with steering or stability is felt while driving. Right away the tyres can be checked for a loss of pressure and the cause of any problem investigated.

When carrying out the routine pressure check, look for any physical damage to the tyres, and stones trapped in the tread – which should be removed. Do not rely on the compressed-air supply at a fuel station for a pressure check as the gauges are notoriously inaccurate. Invest in a high-quality dial-type pressure gauge and get a tread depth gauge too. This is invaluable for checking the wear rates on your tyres. The TT will generally wear out its front tyres quicker than the rears, and rotating the tyres around can even out the wear.

The type of tyres fitted will have a bearing on how you can rotate them. The tyres on family cars can be run at any wheel position and can be rotated around the car, swapping them diagonally. However, many high performance tyres are 'directional'. This means they have been designed to run in one direction only and to place them on the opposite side of the car would make them run backwards, degrading their performance and affecting the car's stability. Only by having a tyre fitter remove, reverse and refit them on the rim, can this be done. Clearly too complex a solution for most owners.

However, directional tyres may be swapped front to rear on the same side of the car, and this would even-out the front-to-rear difference in wear rates. It is worth carrying out this procedure at intervals of between 5,000 and 10,000 miles, depending on the individual car's wear rates.

You will have to utilise the space-saver temporary spare wheel supplied with four-cylinder TTs to achieve this, using it to 'follow' each change around the car. It becomes more complicated, on V6 models – or four-cylinder cars in certain markets – as there is no spare wheel, but a sealing kit to repair the punctured tyre. Here, you will need professional equipment such as axle stands and a greater

You might have to use the temporary spare to assist in tyre rotation. . . (Spectrum Media)

level of knowledge on this type of work. Do not, under any circumstances, attempt to do this if you do not have experience in this area. It might be better simply to request that the Audi workshop carries this out for you.

Equalising the wear on the tyres not only ensures you get the full life out of your tyres, it also means that you replace all four at the same time. Although this

Above: . . . unless, that is, you manage to get a little help from your friends! (LAT)

Below: The V6 cars have no spare wheel but a repair kit instead. Make sure you know how to use it. (Spectrum Media)

means a bigger single expenditure, it is of benefit since, as tyre technology improves all the time the car would otherwise have two tyres of a potentially different level of performance to the other two. Different brands of tyre, or even different ages or technologies of the same brand, will vary in their performance. It is better to have all four tyres of equal performance. Only then, will you get the full benefits that the quattro four-wheel drive and the electronic traction control systems can offer, not to mention their

Below and right: Keep the soft-top and its mechanism clean for best performance. Lubricate carefully if required. (Spectrum Media)

associated ABS and ESP systems which assist in emergencies.

All systems go

None of the TT's systems need any kind of maintenance or specific deference in the way the car is driven. The ABS warning light will illuminate when the ignition is switched on, and then extinguish when the engine has started. On occasions you may hear the pressure pump for the ABS system run – a low rumble – just for a couple of seconds. This is normal, particularly as the car first moves away after it has been parked for a long time. If the ABS warning light comes on while driving, it

indicates a fault; the brakes will work as normal, but without the anti-lock facility. If the light then extinguishes after the engine is started on the next occasion, it could merely have been an error in the system's self-check. However, if such an intermittent warning persists, have the car checked by the Audi workshop. Do this immediately if the light is illuminated constantly.

As some TTs are not the primary car of the household they may stand idle for extended periods. If you cannot remember when you last checked the oil, tyres etc., then do it before the car runs the next time. One system on the car which can remain idle for long periods in temperate-climate regions is the climate control. This should be run at least once a month no matter what the weather conditions. The clutch which engages the compressor drive from the engine can seize if not operated and the pump itself will have a longer life if it is run on a regular basis.

Do not think of the climate control as just a hot-weather item. In cold or wet weather the dehumidified air it provides is infinitely better at demisting the inside of the car than just using the outside air, and used this way throughout the year it will benefit all the climate control system's components.

Visibility in bad weather is also dependent on the state of the windscreen wiper blades. You can check these frequently, but you'll be in no doubt when one is worn or ripped as it will be quite obvious from the poor job it does of clearing the screen. The most common cause of damage is when the rubber blades freeze onto the windscreen in winter. De-ice effectively, as merely trying to pull the blade free will rip it.

The winter weather can take its toll on the Roadster's soft-top too if it is not correctly protected. There are a number of proprietary cleaners and treatments for soft-tops and all do basically what they claim. It is more important to merely keep the hood clean, particularly during the summer months when it will be repeatedly folded and erected. This is important, as large amounts of dust and grit on the fabric will cause abrasions to the surface. Check the operation of the hood folding mechanism too and lubricate it if required. A small amount of white grease from a spray applicator is best for this, but use it sparingly and wipe away any excess. Take care not to allow it to get on the roof fabric itself.

Always use the soft-top cover once the roof is folded, to protect it and the mechanism. (Spectrum Media)

When the roof is folded down, always fit the protective cover. Not only does this make the TT Roadster look a lot more tidy, it prevents dust or debris from becoming trapped in the folds of the fabric top or the operating mechanism. The soft-top should be operated periodically, even if the car is mainly driven with the roof in place. This will ensure the mechanism is kept in good working order. The same applies to the air deflector rear screen, which should also be operated on a regular basis.

Polished performer

Keeping your TT clean is not just about conveying your, or your car's, image. Regularly washed and waxed paintwork will better withstand all that nature and man-made pollutants can throw at it. However, you can clean modern car paints too much. If you own a new TT then the process is one of simple maintenance. If you have a second-hand TT which is not at its best, then the process is one of minor restoration. In either case, take care not to overdo things.

On a new vehicle regular washing and waxing is a good routine to get into. Wash away loose dirt first with a hose-mounted brush ensuring a good through-flow of water, and then wash the bodywork by hand with a sponge and a proprietary car shampoo. Never use any form of household or industrial cleaner on the TT's paintwork, trim or plastics, as irreparable damage can result. Hose the underside of the TT too, particularly after the winter period when the car has run on salted roads. A power wash unit with a long-reach lance is useful for this but take care not to force water at high pressure into joints or seals, and be extra vigilant around the seals and closure faces of windows against the Roadster's soft-top.

Alloy wheels can become soiled with brake pad dust, but these can normally be cleaned with the same products used on the bodywork. Only resort to proprietary wheel-cleaning products if the wheels are heavily soiled. If using on a second-hand TT you have recently bought pay close attention to the instructions for such products' use as such cleaners can be too aggressive on painted alloy finishes, so use sparingly. After use, always wax or polish the wheels to reapply the protective coat which the wheel cleaner will obviously have removed.

The cover is stowed in the boot. (Spectrum Media)

Above: The TT's alloy wheels are painted and should only be subjected to chemical cleaners if very badly soiled with brake pad dust. (Spectrum Media)

Right: Petrol removes wax and polish, so always take care when refuelling. (Spectrum Media)

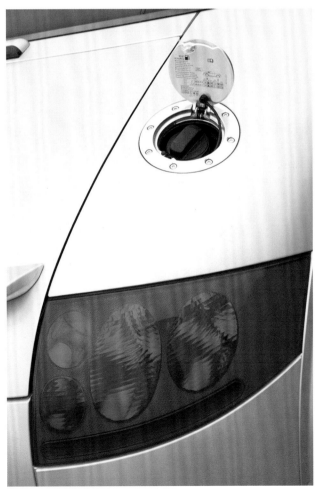

The Roadster's soft-top needs particular treatment. It can be washed with the normal car bodywork shampoo, but it will look better and last longer if cleaned with a good water-repellent soft-top treatment. Normal car shampoo dries to become white in the grain of the fabric, giving the roof a grey and faded look. A soft-top treatment will restore its colour and protect it against staining from bird droppings, which are acidic. Always clean off such deposits from roof or bodywork as soon as possible, even if the car itself is not to be washed. The acidity attacks most car waxes and polishes. Never fold down the soft-top while it is wet. If you need to run the car in open-top form after washing it, drive the first few miles with the roof up to dry it off.

Only polish the car infrequently. If waxed regularly from new, a TT may only need to be polished once per year if garaged, and although a used car might benefit from an initial polishing, be careful not to polish too often. Only use harsher products such as paint renovator or restorer if absolutely necessary as these products contain very fine abrasive particles and are specifically designed to remove a micro-thin layer of paint, clearing away dirty or oxidised finishes to reveal the new paint beneath. Use them with caution if trying to remove a scratch or other blemish. Remember, a scratch only disappears when a thickness of paint the depth of the scratch has been removed. Deep scratches will not polish out and will have to be touched-in with paint.

Soft centre

The interior too needs to be maintained to keep it in top condition. Loose dust can be removed easily by vacuum cleaner and for facia or seats always fit a soft brush tool to prevent scratching. Leather seats need treating occasionally and proprietary leather care products are available. If the car is new only use a conditioner, not a deep cleaner. Unless the leather is badly soiled there is no need for a deep cleaner and this might have the effect of removing some of the treatments carried out by the seat manufacturer. Always condition leather after heavy cleaning.

The leather in modern cars has an enemy close at hand. Climate control systems and air-conditioning units dehumidify the air in the cabin. This removes much of the natural moisture in the air and can

contribute to the leather becoming too dry, particularly if it is not treated regularly in the first place.

All the TT's aluminium interior surfaces should be merely dusted to remove finger marks. Do not use any kind of metal polish on them since they are lacquered and such an abrasive treatment will damage, or even completely remove, the lacquer. At most, use a car bodywork polish suitable for metallic paint – which you will have for the car's exterior finish – and use carefully on interior metallic surfaces. Only use a proprietary facia and interior trim cleaner on the plastic parts of the TTs interior. Never use household chemical cleaners or any kind of solvent on the interior. Any reaction with the interior materials will cause irreversible colour fading.

Of course, one of the biggest causes of colour fading in any fabric or similar material is sunlight. Direct sunlight for lengthy periods will cause rapid drying of the TT's leather and interior trim. This is particularly relevant to the Roadster, and parking in direct sunlight with the roof down is not the best way to keep the leather looking good. Unfortunately, the times in which

Top-down parking can fade the interior. If the car is parked in the sun, put the roof up. (Spectrum Media)

we live mean that there is often little opportunity to leave the car in open mode due to security concerns anyway, but even when parked in a secure environment, consider the image value of leaving your TT Roadster topless, against the potential damage to its interior. Bird droppings don't do much good to your seats either, or your best suit should they go unnoticed on your return.

On the TT Coupé it is worth using a windscreen shade if the car is parked for long periods in strong sunlight. Not only will this protect the interior from UV radiation but will also ensure that the leather seats do not become uncomfortably hot on your return to the car.

At the other extreme of temperature, never attempt to fold down the roof of the TT Roadster if it is frosty or frozen, as the flexibility of the fabric will have been impaired. In extreme cases it might even place too great a loading on the motors used for the electrical operation of the roof. It will not take many minutes before the heater has warmed the interior of the car sufficiently that the frost will have turned to water, allowing the roof to be folded. However, bear in mind that the roof should be raised back into place once more and allowed

to dry properly. Do not leave the roof folded down for long periods if it is wet, but never attempt to dry the roof fabric rapidly by applying any kind of heat to it.

The TT at rest

As a luxury sports car, the TT Coupé and Roaster models are often not the only car in the household, and as such are used as pleasure vehicles rather than daily workhorses. If your TT is used infrequently then a good routine of checks and maintenance should be applied. For a car which tends to be used mainly at the weekend, no special procedures are required. Merely check all the fluid levels in the engine bay and the tyre pressures once per week and allow the engine and transmission a few miles to warm up before utilising the TT's performance. Consider how you would react if you had been in bed all week and someone expected you to get out and immediately run five miles!

For TTs which are used less frequently, or even laid up over the winter months, then a more involved regime should be followed. If the car is cleaned before

The V6 car's battery is under the boot floor. Keep it charged if the car is idle for long periods. (Spectrum Media)

Don't leave the rear seats folded when not carrying anything as this can crease the leather. (Spectrum Media)

being laid up, then ensure it is properly dry. In a garage or car port with good ventilation this is less of a problem, but if the car is to be covered, a great deal of moisture from condensation can form on its metal surfaces. Use a cover which is breathable. These are designed for the long-term storage of classic cars and, although more expensive than a simple dust cover, they are essential if the car is to be idle for some time. In garages a thin dust cover is all that's required, but check periodically for condensation and keep the building well ventilated.

Over a long period of time the car's battery will begin to lose its charge and this must be considered. There are a number of proprietary units on the market which supply a small charge to the battery via a transformer from the mains electrical supply. Although these units offer a sophisticated monitoring system to ensure the battery is not over-charged, there is no substitute for running the car's engine instead. Naturally this too charges the battery, but also keeps the engine in good health. Run the engine once every two weeks if the car is laid up over the winter. Carry out all the engine bay checks before it is started and ensure that the building in which is kept is well ventilated. Exhaust emissions represent a serious health hazard in a confined space, and insufficient ventilation can prove fatal. Never run the engine in a confined space without a good level of through-flow ventilation to evacuate the fumes. It is far better to bring the car out into the open, especially as this also turns all the drive line components too. Bring the engine up to operating temperature and vary the engine speed slightly as it warms, but do not rev the engine hard. Operate the air-conditioning unit too, and the electric motors such as those powering the windows and the soft-top on Roadster models.

If the car is laid up for long periods you will be able to reduce your insurance costs. Speak to your insurer about off-the-road cover, and ensure that you are still fully covered for theft, fire and accidental damage. Remember to get the full cover reinstated before the

car is run on the road again. You can only reduce the level of cover if the car is stored off the public highway. However, your Audi TT was made for driving and it will be in the best of health if it is used regularly. If the car has to be stored for a long period without being run, consult your Audi Centre for their advice on long term storage.

Tuning and modifying a TT

When most owners think of modifications to their car, they generally think of more engine power. Engine modifications, it is true, can totally transform a standard car, but they can also ruin it. In motorsport the best development engineers seldom give the car as much power as possible and then try to make the chassis cope. They work the other way around and develop the chassis first, before giving the car the maximum power the chassis can then use. Witness the TT itself. Audi does not make a front-wheel-drive TT with the 225PS turbo engine, or the 3.2-litre V6. Certainly such cars would have an equally high maximum speed compared to the quattro versions which use these engines and once the problems of traction from a standing start have been overcome they would accelerate just as strongly. The reason Audi does not bestow this much power on the front-wheel-drive car, is for the simple reason that it is too much to achieve a fine handling balance and good all-round drivability. Remember this simple and unavoidable fact when considering modifications to your TT.

Racing techniques

Like the professional engineers then, we shall look at modifying the TT to take more power, and not find ourselves wondering how to cope with increased power. Cost is obviously a big factor too, and it is fair to say that small investments can make a big difference.

If you have bought a second-hand TT and the tyres are in need of replacement then this can be a cost-effective modification. Why go for a straight-forward replacement set of tyres, when you could, for a small increase in expenditure, fit a higher performance tyre?

Although not as popular for modifying as the hot-hatch, the TT has its fans. (*Max Power*)

Learn from the experts. Racing cars don't have any more power than they can use. (LAT)

There is a culture to merely fit larger tyres, but this is not always of benefit. Fitting a larger diameter wheel, means that you must fit a lower-profile tyre – that is one with a less side wall height – or aspect ratio – to maintain the same overall tyre diameter. If you do not do this, at the very least your speedometer will read incorrectly, you will increase the overall gearing, blunting the car's performance or may even find that the tyres foul and rub on the inside of the wheelarches.

The Audi TT models already use relatively low-profile tyres. Perhaps a better solution might be to go for a directional ultra-high-performance tyre which will improve grip and cornering power. Bear in mind how-ever that higher performance tyres wear out more quickly. There is a culture in the motorcycling world which accepts this and riders of high performance sports motorcycles think nothing of fitting a tyre which might only last two thousand miles in hard riding, as opposed to six thousand miles for a standard tyre. Most car drivers would be horrified to switch to a tyre with only one-third of the normal life, so it's a difficult decision.

Of course, it is a temporary performance improvement. To maintain it you must use high-performance tyres at each replacement cycle and many drivers who have chosen this route revert back to standard tyres next time around, due to cost.

Another level

Nowhere, is compromise more necessary in an all-round road car than in the suspension design. It has to give the expected degree of ride comfort for non-enthusiast owners, but also the level of handling required by those who drive their TT hard. Modifications will shift this compromise towards the more sporting, so should not be undertaken lightly.

The most popular suspension modification is a set of lowered springs. Many popular kits make the TT 20mm lower, and are normally of the progressive rate type of spring. These give a decent level of ride comfort over minor bumps but become gradually stiffer with more movement, to limit body roll.

There are many companies who supply performance suspension and lowering kits, and the popularity of the TT means most have kits for this car.

If you wish to have a say in the way your TT handles from day to day, or indeed wish to use it on

After-market suspension kits can affect the TT's accurate suspension geometry settings. Always make sure the car sits level. (*Max Power*)

the road and the track, then a suspension modification which includes adjustable dampers is the best option.

Merely lowering the car has little merit. Some 'styling' kits reduce the ride height by as much as 35mm (1.4in) but can affect the suspension geometry to the detriment of overall handling. Also consider that the rear springs of the TT quattro are physically very short, and lowering the car here can cause camber changes so acute that it looks as if the car is overloaded, such is the angle of the wheel to the road.

Before even contemplating modifying the suspension have the standard car thoroughly checked – particularly if you bought it second-hand – to ensure that camber, toe-in and castor, are all correct. Any one of these will, if misaligned, affect steering feel and turn-in – the car's ability to rapidly change direction at speed without loss of tyre grip.

Any suspension modification must be allowed some mileage to settle-in. Replacing dampers, springs and associated bushings will all affect the car's ability at first. Do not be tempted to fully test your new suspension set-up in the first mile from the workshop. Ensure also that any modification will not affect your future choice of tyre, this is particularly important with conversions which lower the ride height.

Although suspension modifications are not as popular as the numerous modifications for engine performance, they can in many ways add more to the overall driving pleasure of a car like the TT. The simple fact is that engine modifications only benefit the car in its acceleration or top speed, the latter of which is of very limited use on the roads of today, and even if the owner uses the car on racetrack days, straight-line speed is of limited value overall. Suspension modifications on the other hand, ensure the best performance from the tyres, enhance the braking stability by reducing forward weight transfer, and naturally, improve the cornering ability of the car.

Just as merely lowering the car is of limited benefit, simply stiffening up the suspension is likewise of little use. It is a myth that a car handles better per se, with stiffer suspension. On a very smooth racetrack that may be so, but on the public road it is still very much about compromise and progressive rate strings allied to adjustable dampers, are usually the best all-round option.

Split-rim design wheels like this are favoured for very low profile tyres. (Rage Products)

The final detail in personalisation – tyre valve caps with your car's badge on them. (Rage Products)

Above: Lowered cars cruise smooth roads easily but take care over rough city streets and speed humps. (*Max Power*)

Left: The TT's standard seats are excellent, but racing style seats offer a further personalisation of your TT. (Rage Products)

Right: Larger diameter wheels look good, but ensure you have the correct clearance. Cross-drilled discs like this one offer better brake cooling and hence performance. (*Max Power*)

An abrupt halt

One way to make your TT go faster is to fit upgraded brakes! Improving the braking ability of the car is not the first thing that springs to mind when considering how to make a car faster. The TT already has a very powerful braking system as standard, using components from Audi's 'S' quattro perform-ance saloon cars. However, a brake upgrade is important if you plan to increase the TT's engine power above standard, and in any case, will make the car more rewarding over demanding roads. If you plan to use it on racetrack days, a good fade-free competition-style braking set-up is an excellent idea.

To reduce fade – where rising temperatures reduce retardation – on fast winding roads or racetrack days, many TT owners turn to racing-style Kevlar composite brake pads. In addition to resisting fade at high temperatures, many owners claim an improvement in braking in the wet, where the conventional pad material feels 'wooden' at low temperatures. However, unlike traditional competition pads, the composite types do not need to be pre-faded or have to be constantly at high temperature for full performance. Ensure any you fit are actually intended for road use. Some competition-only materials are not designed for low-temperature road use.

Just replacing the pad material alone might not have a big effect on the car's braking performance. If the pads are ready for renewal in any case, it's a minor increase in cost. If the discs themselves are in good order it seems a waste of money to change them. However, if the discs are worn, or if you wish to get the full benefit from a brake upgrade, new discs are a worthwhile investment. Going this route is normally done by buying discs and pads as a set. Pad material and cross-drilled brake discs – like those on racing cars or high-performance motorcycles – have two advantages.

The grooves or holes allow water to clear easily from the surface of the disc, improving friction with the pads while also preventing the pad from becoming too glazed. Since the pads are designed to work with such discs, worries over increased wear rates are usually unfounded.

There are many makes of kit on the market, and most of these have been designed with a motorsport background. Suppliers will be well-versed in the TT's requirements but always discuss wheel and tyre size with respect to larger discs and of course physical clearances within the wheel. This is where the fitting of wider wheels and tyres on the TT can become troublesome. Fit new brakes to suit optional wheels and you might have a problem with a replacement wheel in the future, or more worrying, the space-saver spare tyre when you come to use it.

On family cars a popular upgrade is to use brakes from the higher performance version of the range. That is not the case with the TT, but many owners – like Ur quattro drivers before them – find that they can upgrade to Porsche brakes. This is not as strange as it first seems, as on the Audi RS2 Avant, Audi themselves used Porsche brakes!

DID YOU KNOW?

A rolling-road tune is worthwhile on a standard car and is the most cost-effective tuning money you'll ever spend.

Road to nowhere

In any form of engine tuning, the final setting should be made on a 'rolling-road'. Only by taking readings from the engine when it is under operating load can the fuel, ignition and turbo-boost be set correctly. The rolling-road tuner can also spot areas of under performance in the engine. Merely having a standard car subjected to a rolling-road test and tune is a good investment, but always ensure your TT is correctly serviced and has no known faults or weaknesses in the engine or driveline. A rolling-road test will find these, sometimes with spectacular and often expensive results. Rolling-road operators do not accept liability for engine damage due to the loading placed upon the car during the test.

Although the front-wheel-drive TT can be tuned on a standard rolling road, the quattro cars need to be run on a four-wheel rolling road. However, anyone specialising in either Audi or specifically quattro modifications, will have such a device.

Before considering any kind of engine modification, ensure that all the components of the TT are in good order – particularly if you have bought the car second-hand. Replace the air filter, fuel filter

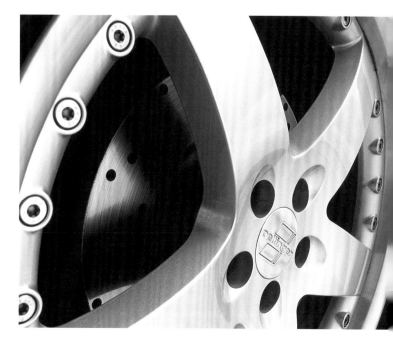

and spark plugs if you are uncertain of their age and check all pipes, hoses and leads connected with these systems, the turbo wastegate settings and exhaust system for faults. A thorough resetting of all the TT's systems can often release more power if the car was not running at full strength in the first instance.

Getting around the map

The widespread use of electronics in the control of engines has caused people to believe that retuning them is merely down to a few clicks of a computer mouse. The truth is rather more complicated, and the parameters for increasing engine performance have not actually changed. The electronics only

If your engine is highly tuned, fit oil pressure and temperature gauges to keep an eye on it. A turbo boost gauge might be of use too. (*Max Power*)

control the engine. The amount of air, fuel and the timing of the ignition spark all have the same values relative to each other as they always have done. To get more power you burn more fuel, in more air. Where once it was a case of modifying the carburettors, inlet tract and exhaust system, it is now a matter of modifying the systems which control fuel, air and ignition.

Before considering any form of engine modification to increase your TT's power, consider whether you have upgraded the suspension or brakes accordingly. A little extra punch for safe overtaking is fine, but always remember that if it allows safe overtaking in a shorter length of straight road, you will arrive at the next corner at a higher speed. Don't become power crazed.

Remapping of the engine management ECU, which controls all the engine functions of ignition timing, fuel injection and turbo boost pressure, is used to get more power.

For more fuel to be burnt, more air is required in the cylinders. On a naturally aspirated engine this can mean a bigger inlet tract, bigger valves and even modification of the cylinder head to increase the compression ratio. On a turbocharged engine, raising the turbo's boost pressure produces the same result. Here lies the danger. It is all too easy to turn up the boost by too much, threatening reliability of the turbo unit and the engine itself.

If done in moderation, more power can be safely generated by the engine. However, it has to be remembered that in standard form the 225PS engine has a number of physical differences from the 180PS, so the owner should not take Audi's tendency to over-engineer its cars too far. The TT is not indestructible. You should also change the oil more frequently and generally service the car more often. The variable service system is not designed to account for modified engines.

Remapping gains can be significant in the TT with the 180PS engine's output being increased to over 200PS and the 225PS engine up to 250PS. This is an average figure from a number of different remapping suppliers. Some companies go further and make huge power claims merely from changing the map, but you need to bear in mind reliability. Sure, back in the Group B rally days, quattros whose engines produced a 'mere' 200bhp in road trim, were being tuned to over 500bhp for rallying. However, they would often require a new turbocharger unit each day of the rally, and if the engine made it to the end of the event at all, it would probably be scrapped on its return to Ingolstadt. Hardly the best operating profile for a private car!

Much of the trend for tuning and remapping the TT's turbocharged engine stems from the days of the quattro. Although the road-going quattro will be recorded by historians for its use of four-wheel drive in a performance car, in actual fact it did more to advance the cause of the turbocharger during its life. With the benefits of adjustable boost and intercooling

Above: Racing style pedals are simple components to fit and can be colour coded to the car or interior. (Rage Products)

Below: Even the TT can benefit from more power and performance but don't exceed the limits of the handling and braking. (Max Power)

Above: The carbon look, popular in the modified field, has extended from the cockpit to external components such as the exhaust. (Rage Products)

Below: A leather gearshift gaiter adds a touch more style than the TT's standard rubberised item. (Rage Products)

The scene was set and with widespread use of turbocharging and electronic engine management in the quattros through 10 and 20-valve Ur quattro models, the S2, the big 200 quattro and RS2 Avant guises, they become firm favourites with German and UK tuning houses.

For bigger power increases today, you are not merely into the remapping of the engine, but the rebuilding of it. Specialist companies undertaking such work will rebuild the engine with stronger pistons and connecting rods, even a competition grade crankshaft, lightened flywheel and modified cylinder head with larger valves. This is serious work and not to be confused with a retuning of the engine. Power gains here are large, almost double that of the standard engine and are in no way suitable for a TT with standard suspension and brakes.

The other side of the story

If you consider that changes to fuel and ignition, cylinder head and turbo modifications tend to *force* the engine to produce more power, then exhaust modifications surely *allow* it to produce more power.

The exhaust system on any car creates a restriction to the flow of gas from the engine. This much is obvious to anyone who has experienced a cracked or split exhaust system on an older car when the engine idle speed increases significantly of its own accord. If the exhaust is leaking before the silencer components, the effect is greatest. Modern engines tend to reset their idle speed in such an instance so the resistance created by the exhaust is not as obvious to drivers of more modern cars, as it once was.

It has long been a popular modification to petrol engines of all types, to fit a performance exhaust. This is designed to allow a better flow of gases from the engine and should not be confused with merely a larger bore tail pipe, generally fitted to increase or change the sound of the exhaust for purely image reasons.

Given that the power output and the accelerative ability of a turbocharged engine is linked to the speed at which the turbocharger can spin up to full speed, then the flow of exhaust gas will have a direct bearing upon it. In theory then, a free-flow exhaust is of even more benefit to a turbo engine than it is to a naturally aspirated one. Partly this is true, but there are also considerations of turbo back pressure to create the correct loading upon the exhaust turbine, or to prevent it from over speed running.

which Audi developed in rallying, they were able to tame the unruly behaviour which had until then, been the hallmark of the turbocharged petrol engine. Although Saab and Renault carried out a lot of development, the previous German effort – the BMW 2002 Turbo – was turbo-lag personified, changing character rapidly as the turbo's effect kicked in.

Many TT owners and those specialising in the tuning of the TT's turbocharged range of engines cite one particular problem. There is an obvious restriction where the exhaust system has to clear the Haldex coupling and rear differential in the quattro cars. A number of companies produce a racing-style stainless-steel system with a larger bore pipe and a modified routing around the rear differential unit, which, it is claimed, removes a restriction on the exhaust gas flow.

A further option is to replace the standard catalytic converter with a high-flow unit. These generally take the form of a catalytic converter with a lower density substrate – the tightly packed core of the converter which filters the exhaust gases – allowing the exhaust gas to flow more freely. The downside is that emission legislation varies around the world and a modification suitable for one market, may not allow the TT to maintain its original emission controls in another. Further claims for a lower heat absorption by the substrate is another benefit of free-flow converters, but you should check the legality of the emissions in individual markets for which the replacement converters were originally designed.

The benefits of increasing, or easing the exhaust gas flow are real enough, and the testing of such systems has shown gains of up to 5 per cent more power and as much as 10 per cent more torque, no doubt from the turbocharger spinning up to full operating pressure a little earlier.

Cool it

It is something of an oversimplification to say that increasing the turbo-boost pressure of the engine increases the power. Merely increasing the pressure is not sufficient; what the engineers are aiming to do is increase its mass. Basically, power only comes from the amount – or mass – of fuel having the correct mass of air in which to burn. To increase the mass of air in a fixed volume the air is compressed, to increase its density. These are the fundamentals of supercharging, which go back to the early 1900s.

However, as the air is compressed, it increases in temperature too, reducing its density. This is the function of the intercooler. Cooling the compressed air gives it a greater density once more and the natural progression for anyone tuning the TT's turbocharged engine is to increase the efficiency of the intercooler.

The 180PS engine has one intercooler, the 225PS engine has two. They are mounted in the inner wing of the TT close to the wheelarch. This means that although they gain a good air flow at high speed, and from relatively close to the ground, a front-mounted intercooler would be preferable.

However, the popular modification of fitting a larger intercooler in the front of the TT's engine bay is not without its problems. The standard coolant radiator, oil cooler and evaporator for the climate control, all jostle for space behind the TT's air intakes. The front-mounted intercooler has to be of a very open matrix design to prevent a restriction – and hence starvation – of cool air to the other heat exchangers. Moreover, it cannot appreciably increase the air temperature flowing into the other radiators, for obvious reasons. A larger intercooler is worth considering on an otherwise standard, or slightly remapped car, but really it only covers its cost implication when tuning to higher boost pressures.

The top of the scale as regards engine tuning on the four-cylinder turbocharged TT engine is the fitting of a larger turbocharger.

This should only be considered in conjunction with new manifolds, wastegate, free flow exhaust system, a reprogramming of the ECU and considerable internal engine modifications, to cope with the increased power. Here, fitting a larger intercooler will be essential.

For such conversions companies are claiming as much as 320PS from a 180PS or 225PS starting point. Although such power outputs give the TT supercar levels of acceleration, such as 0–100kph (0–62mph) in 5.5 seconds, it must be remembered that the transmission system in the TT is only designed for the power and torque of the 250PS V6 engine currently. Also, considerable upgrades to braking and suspension will be required if the car is not to become unrewarding or even hazardous to drive.

Above left: Carbon components lend a racing car feel and items like gear knobs are easy to fit. (Rage Products)

Above: Colour coding can extend to the engine bay. This is an oil filter cap, note the indendation design, matching the TT's interior styling cues. (Rage Products)

Left: The interior is the part of the car the driver sees most of all, therefore many people consider it the most important area of the car. (*Max Power*)

Right: Performance air filters increase engine breathing, and can be colour matched to your car too. (Rage Products)

Modifications of the 3.2-litre V6 engine are far less reliant on remapping than they are for a turbo engine and here the skills of engine building come to the fore once more, with extensive physical modifications required to extract any large gains in power. However, turbocharging the V6 is already an option and claims of over 400PS are made for such conversions.

Remember to inform your insurers of any modification to your TT. Failure to do so might invalidate your insurance cover.

Body beautiful

One of Freeman Thomas's 1994 sketches of the 'low-drag coupé' is captioned with the words that all age groups, men and women, should feel like 'wearing this coupé'. For those who need to feel that they 'wear' their TT, just as importantly as drive it, modifications to the body and general aesthetics come to prominence.

It is perhaps somewhat perverse that a car which has been hailed by those with no deep interest in cars themselves, as a design icon, should then be the focus of so much body addenda and modification. However, this is the case.

Some of the body modifications have a practical purpose. Larger rear spoilers and deeper front airdams can contribute to better straight-line stability at high speed and are perhaps welcome by those applying larger, even excessive, amounts of power to the TT's chassis. Indeed, Audi itself had to modify the TT's aerodynamic package in the early days, due to fears of high-speed instability, after some accidents on German autobahns.

With the TT's standard styling, deep front spoiler and very wraparound lines to the wheelarches, there is little scope to offer a full body kit as one would find for a performance hatchback. The TT already hugs the road, and attempting to lower its lines still further bring expensive panels close to any large irregularities in the road. Ramps and underground car parks can present their own problems too, so combining body styling components with suspension lowering kits can prove impractical.

Lower door-edge finishing components and full sill skirts offer some protection from stones thrown up by the front wheels and this can be particularly relevant if wider tyres are fitted.

Deeper front airdams generally also feature a larger intake 'mouth' to keep the TT's look in proportion and will assist considerably if the car has been fitted with a larger front-mounted intercooler as part of an engine tuning package.

However, a deeper front airdam can considerably reduce the amount of air flow beneath the car. Normally this is beneficial, but it can also change the air-flow

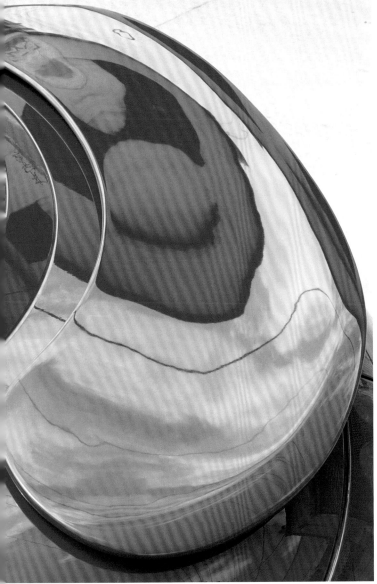

over the TT's undertray aerodynamic aids. For this reason it should always be combined with a larger rear spoiler to maintain aerodynamic balance.

Safe and sound

Unfortunately, such modifications also make your TT more attractive to others, and modified cars can often be targeted by thieves for their expensive modifications alone, over and above the desirability of the TT itself.

Although the TT is fitted with the latest generation of electronic immobilisers it is often worthwhile to take further security measures.

Tracking devices are often favoured by insurance companies on high-performance cars such as the TT. These accurately report the car's position to a centralised control centre allowing police vehicles and helicopters equipped with suitable tracking signal devices to home-in on the car's current location. Such devices serve as a good deterrent against professional criminals who will expect to sell the car or possibly break it for parts.

Remote smart card systems are another useful development. If the car is taken with the key in and engine already running, the smart card – which is carried on the driver's person and not kept in the car – cuts the engine after a brief period when its trans-

The TT's lines are not eye-catching enough for some, and aftermarket body adornments and different rear spoilers abound. (*Max Power*)

mission range is exceeded. So the thief will not get more than a mile away before the engine cuts out and the car is immobilised.

A whole book could be written on the various types of ICE equipment that is available. The TT's standard system is a radio/cassette, although few cars leave the showroom without the upgrade to a radio/single CD player.

The obvious further option of a six-disc autochanger is equally common, particularly on higher specification cars. A Bose system with increased amplifier power and high-grade speakers is the top option and using this as a basis for further upgrades is a natural progression.

The car with the smaller cabin, the TT Roadster is probably more suited to personal customisation in this area. The well into which the roof folds, and two cubby slots behind the seats offer potential positions for additional speakers, although using the roof well has its limitations once insulated by several layers of folded soft-top.

So, modifications for the TT are every bit as varied, and easy to tailor to individual needs as the TT itself. It appeals to different owners for different reasons. For its looks, its performance or its heritage and history. Add in the factory options, accessories and huge range of aftermarket modifications and it is easy to see why people love the TT so much. Although they share common components, each car represents different values for its owner. Only the link is truly unique. The link between you, and your Audi TT.

75mm soft aluminum tube

Aluminum Intake funel

sizes - 50, 75, 100mm
2", 3", 4"

Above: Custom ICE is a world in itself – from a simple factory option upgrade to filling the entire luggage space. (*Max Power*)

Left: Open air intakes are intended purely for competition use, but large tubes can be used for increased engine breathing. (*Rage Products*)

Appendix A

Specifications

Roadsters

150

ENGINE/ELECTRICS

Engine type	4-cylinder spark-ignition engine with exhaust-gas turbocharger and intercooler, DOHC
Displacement	1,781cc
Max. output	110kw (150PS) at 5,700rpm
Max. torque	155lb ft (210Nm) at 1,750–4,600rpm
Engine management	Motronic ME 7.5
Emission control system	Heated oxygen sensor, activated carbon filter, 3-way catalytic converter.

DRIVELINE

Type	Front-wheel drive with traction control anti-slip regulation system (ASR)
Clutch	Hydraulically operated single-plate dry clutch
Gearbox	5-speed manual gearbox

SUSPENSION/BRAKING

Front axle	MacPherson struts with lower wishbones, subframe, anti-roll bar
Rear axle	Torsion-beam rear suspension, tubular anti-roll bar
Brake system	Dual-circuit brake system with diagonal split; anti-lock braking system (ABS)/electronic brake-force distribution (EBD) with electronic stability programme (ESP) and brake assist, brake servo; front: ventilated discs/rear: discs

WHEELS
7J x 16 '7-spoke' alloys

STEERING
Power-assisted, maintenance-free rack-and-pinion

WEIGHTS/VOLUMES

Unladen weight	1,335kg
Gross weight limit	1,635kg
Tank capacity	55 litres

PERFORMANCE DATA/FUEL CONSUMPTION

Top speed	133mph
Acceleration, 0–62mph	8.9sec

AUDIO/COMMUNICATION
Chorus RDS radio/cassette

EXTERIOR
Electrically adjustable glass wind deflector
Electrically powered soft-top
Fully zinc galvanised body
Heat insulating tinted glass

INTERIOR
Driver's information system (DIS)
Dust and pollen filter
Electric front windows
Electronic climate control
Outside temperature gauge

SAFETY/TECHNOLOGY
Adjustable steering column (height/depth)
Anti-theft device with interior ultrasonic protection
Driver and front passenger airbags

Electric headlight adjustment
Electrically heated windscreen washer jets
Electrically operated and heated door mirrors
Electronic anti-lock braking system (ABS)
Electronic brake-force distribution (EBD)
Electronic differential lock (EDL) – traction control
Electronic stability programme (ESP)
Ellipsoidal headlamps
Front passenger airbag isolation
Front side airbags (head and thorax)
Power steering
Remote central locking (radio wave) with folding key
Side impact protection
Space-saver spare wheel
Transponder immobiliser
Twin aluminium rollover protection hoops
Visible vehicle identification number

SEATS
Front sports seats
Height adjustable front seats

STEERING WHEEL
Sports leather

Options

AUDIO/COMMUNICATION
BOSE sound system

CD autochanger
Concert II radio
GSM mobile telephone preparation
Satellite navigation system

EXTERIOR
Metallic/pearl effect paints
Special order colours

INTERIOR
Cruise control
Alcantara/leather combination
Fine Nappa leather
Moccasin leather
Red/Silver leather

SAFETY/TECHNOLOGY
Headlight washers
Lowered sports suspension
Xenon headlights

SEATS
Heated front seats

WHEELS
7.5J x 17 'competition-design' alloy wheels with 225/45 R17 tyres
7.5J x 17 '6-arm' design alloy wheels with 225/45 R17 tyres
8J x 18 'cross-spoke' design alloy wheels with 225/40 ZR18Y tyres
8J x 18 '9-spoke' design alloy wheels with 225/40 ZR18Y tyres

180

ENGINE/ELECTRICS

Engine type	4-cylinder inline, spark ignition, 5-valve technology, exhaust-gas turbocharger, double overhead camshaft (DOHC)
Displacement	1,781cc
Max. output	132kW (180PS) at 5,500rpm
Max. torque	173lb ft (235Nm) at 1,950–5,000rpm
Engine management	Motronic, air-mass measurement, charge air cooling.
Emission control system	3-way catalytic converter, heated Lambda sensor, active carbon filter

DRIVELINE

Type	Permanent four-wheel drive, ASR, EDL – traction control, electronic stability programme ESP with 'brake-assist'
Gearbox	6-speed manual, synchromesh on all ratios including reverse

SUSPENSION/BRAKING

Front axle	MacPherson struts with lower wishbones, anti-roll bar
Rear axle	Double wishbone, track-correcting bearings, anti-roll bar
Brake system	Dual-circuit brake system with diagonal split, ABS with EBD, discs front and rear, ventilated front discs

WHEELS
8J x 18 '9-spoke' alloys

STEERING

Power-assisted, maintenance-free rack-and-pinion, track-stabilising
steering roll radius, turning circle approx. 10.48m

PERFORMANCE DATA

Top speed	137mph
Acceleration, 0–62mph	8.2sec

WEIGHTS/VOLUMES

Unladen weight	1,466kg
Gross weight limit	1,765kg
Tank capacity	62 litres

225

ENGINE/ELECTRICS

Engine type	4-cylinder inline, spark ignition, 5-valve technology, exhaust-gas turbocharger, double overhead camshaft (DOHC)
Displacement	1,781cc
Max. output	165kW (225PS) at 5,090rpm
Max. torque	207lb ft (280Nm) at 2,200–5,500rpm
Engine management	Motronic, air-mass measurement, charge air cooling
Emission control system	3-way catalytic converter, heated lambda sensor, active carbon filter

DRIVELINE

Type	Permanent four-wheel drive, ASR, EDL – traction control, ESP with 'brake-assist'
Gearbox	6-speed manual, synchromesh on all ratios including reverse

SUSPENSION/BRAKING

Front axle	MacPherson struts with lower wishbones, anti-roll bar
Rear axle	Double wishbone, track correcting bearings, anti-roll bar
Brake system	Dual-circuit brake system with diagonal split, ABS with EBD, ventilated front and rear discs

WHEELS

8J x 18 '9-spoke' alloys

STEERING

Power-assisted, maintenance-free rack-and-pinion, track stabilising steering
roll radius, turning circle approx. 10.48m

WEIGHTS/VOLUMES

Unladen weight	1,515kg
Gross weight limit	1,815kg
Tank capacity	62 litres

PERFORMANCE DATA

Top speed	147mph
Acceleration, 0–62mph	6.9sec

V6 3.2 Manual

ENGINE/ELECTRICS

Engine type	Six-cylinder spark-ignition engine, DOHC
Displacement	3,189cc
Max. output	184kW (250PS) at 6,300rpm
Max. torque	236lb ft (320Nm) at 2,800–3,200rpm
Engine management	Motronic ME 7.1.1

DRIVELINE

Type	Quattro permanent four-wheel drive with electronically controlled multi-plate clutch, EDL, ESP
Gearbox	6-speed manual gearbox, synchromesh on all gears

SUSPENSION/BRAKING

Front axle	MacPherson struts with lower wishbones, subframe, anti-roll bar
Rear axle	Longitudinal double wishbones, subframe, anti-roll bar, gas-filled shock absorbers
Brake system	Dual-circuit brake system with diagonal split, ABS/EBD, brake servo, ventilated brake discs at front and rear, front: 17in dual-piston high-performance brakes

WHEELS
7.5J x 18 '7-spoke' alloys

STEERING
Power-assisted, maintenance-free rack-and-pinion steering

WEIGHTS/VOLUMES	
Unladen weight	1,560kg
Gross weight limit	1,860kg
Tank capacity	62 litres

PERFORMANCE DATA	
Top speed	155mph
Acceleration, 0–62mph	6.7sec

V3.2 DSG

ENGINE/ELECTRICS

Engine type	Six-cylinder spark-ignition engine, DOHC
Displacement	3,189cc
Max. output	184kW (250PS) at 6,300rpm
Max. torque	236lb ft (320Nm) at 2,800–3,200rpm
Engine management	Motronic ME 7.1.1

DRIVELINE

Type	Quattro permanent four-wheel drive with electronically controlled multi-plate clutch, EDL, ESP
Gearbox	6-speed DSG with electro-hydraulic control

SUSPENSION/BRAKING

Front axle	MacPherson struts with lower wishbones, subframe, anti-roll bar
Rear axle	Longitudinal double wishbones, subframe, anti-roll bar, gas-filled shock absorbers
Brake system	Dual-circuit brake system with diagonal split, ABS/EBD, brake servo, ventilated brake discs at front and rear, front: 17in dual-piston high-performance brakes

WHEELS
7.5J x 18 '7-spoke' alloys

STEERING
Power-assisted, maintenance-free rack-and-pinion

WEIGHTS/VOLUMES	
Unladen weight	1,590kg
Gross weight limit	1,890kg
Tank capacity	62 litres

PERFORMANCE DATA	
Top speed	155mph
Acceleration, 0–62mph	6.6sec

Coupés

180

ENGINE/ELECTRICS

Engine type	4-cylinder inline, spark ignition, 5-valve technology, exhaust-gas turbocharger, double overhead camshaft (DOHC)
Displacement	1,781cc
Max. output	132kW (180PS) at 5,500rpm
Max. torque	173lb ft (235Nm) at 1,950–5,000rpm
Engine management	Motronic, air-mass measurement, charge air cooling

DRIVELINE

Type	Permanent four-wheel drive, ASR, EDL – traction control, ESP with 'brake-assist'
Gearbox	6-speed manual, synchromesh on all ratios including reverse

SUSPENSION/BRAKING

Front axle	MacPherson struts with lower wishbones, anti-roll bar
Rear axle	Double wishbone, track correcting bearings, anti-roll bar
Brake system	Dual-circuit brake system with diagonal split, ABS with EBD, discs front and rear, ventilated front discs

WHEELS
8J x 18 '9-spoke' alloys

STEERING
Power-assisted, maintenance-free rack-and-pinion, track-stabilising
steering roll radius, turning circle approx. 10.45m

WEIGHTS/VOLUMES

Unladen weight	1,410kg
Gross weight limit	1,795kg
Tank capacity	62 litres

PERFORMANCE DATA

Top speed	140mph
Acceleration, 0–62mph	7.9sec

225

ENGINE/ELECTRICS

Engine type	4-cylinder inline, spark ignition, 5-valve technology, exhaust-gas turbocharger, double overhead camshaft (DOHC)
Displacement	1,781cc
Max. output	165kW (225PS) at 5,900rpm
Max. torque	207lb ft (280Nm) at 2,200–5,500rpm
Engine management	Motronic, air mass measurement, charge air cooling

DRIVELINE

Type	Permanent four-wheel drive, ASR, EDL – traction control, ESP with 'brake-assist'
Gearbox	6-speed manual, synchromesh on all ratios including reverse

SUSPENSION/BRAKING

Front axle	MacPherson struts with lower wishbones, anti-roll bar
Rear axle	Double wishbone, track correcting bearings, anti-roll bar
Brake system	Dual-circuit brake system with diagonal split, ABS with EBD, ventilated front and rear discs

WHEELS
8J x 18 '9-spoke' alloys

STEERING
Power-assisted, maintenance-free rack-and-pinion, track stabilising steering
roll radius, turning circle approx. 10.45m

WEIGHTS/VOLUMES

Unladen weight	1,410kg
Gross weight limit	1,795kg
Tank capacity	62 litres

PERFORMANCE DATA

Top speed	151mph
Acceleration, 0–62mph	6.6sec

V6 3.2 Manual

ENGINE/ELECTRICS

Engine type	Six-cylinder spark-ignition engine, DOHC
Displacement	3,189cc
Max. output	184kW (250PS) at 6,300rpm
Max. torque	236lb ft (320Nm) at 2,800–3,200rpm
Engine management	Motronic ME 7.1.1

DRIVELINE

Type	Quattro permanent four-wheel drive with electronically controlled multi-plate clutch, EDL, ESP
Gearbox	6-speed manual gearbox, synchromesh on all gears

SUSPENSION/BRAKING

Front axle	MacPherson struts with lower wishbones, subframe, anti-roll bar
Rear axle	Longitudinal double wishbones, subframe, anti-roll bar, gas-filled shock absorbers
Brake system	Dual-circuit brake system with diagonal split, ABS/EBD, brake servo, ventilated brake discs at front and rear, front: 17in dual-piston high-performance brakes

WHEELS
7.5J x 18 '7-spoke' alloys

STEERING
Power-assisted, maintenance-free rack-and-pinion

WEIGHTS/VOLUMES

Unladen weight	1,490kg
Gross weight limit	1,875kg
Tank capacity	62 litres

PERFORMANCE DATA

Top speed	155mph
Acceleration, 0–62mph	6.5sec

V6 3.2 DSG

ENGINE/ELECTRICS

Engine type	Six-cylinder spark-ignition engine, DOHC
Displacement	3,189cc
Max. output	184kW (250PS) at 6,300rpm
Max. torque	236lb ft (320Nm) at 2,800–3,200rpm
Engine management	Motronic ME 7.1.1

DRIVELINE

Type	Quattro permanent four-wheel drive with electronically controlled multi-plate clutch, EDL, ESP
Gearbox	6-speed DSG with electro-hydraulic control

SUSPENSION/BRAKING

Front axle	MacPherson struts with lower wishbones, subframe, anti-roll bar
Rear axle	Longitudinal double wishbones, subframe, anti-roll bar, gas-filled shock absorbers
Brake system	Dual-circuit brake system with diagonal split, ABS/EBD, brake servo, ventilated brake discs at front and rear, front: 17in dual-piston high-performance brakes

WHEELS
7.5J x 18 '7-spoke' alloys

STEERING
Power-assisted, maintenance-free rack-and-pinion

WEIGHTS/VOLUMES:

Unladen weight	1,520kg
Gross weight limit	1,905kg
Tank capacity	62 litres

PERFORMANCE DATA

Top speed	155mph
Acceleration, 0–62mph	6.4sec

Appendix B

Useful contacts

Websites:

AUDI CORPORATE:
www.audi.co.uk (official Audi UK site)
www.audi.de (Audi Germany site)
www.audi.de/foren (Museum in Ingolstadt)

AUDI AND TT SPECIFIC SITES:
www.auto-amd.com (engine tuning)
www.abtsportsline.co.uk (styling)
www.dialynx.co.uk (tuning and performance parts)
www.forgemotorsports.co.uk (engine tuning)
www.jabbasport.com (engine tuning and rolling road)
www.milltek.co.uk (performance exhausts)

www.partsforaudi.co.uk (for all Audi parts)
www.powerchips.com (ECU remapping)
www.quattrosports.co.uk (all things quattro)
www.revotechnik.com (ECU remapping)
www.roadsterinsurance.com (insurance for TT)
www.spaxperformance.com (performance suspension)
www.starperformance.co.uk (ECU remapping)
www.thettshop.com (for all things TT)
www.tt-forum.co.uk (for all things TT)
www.tunit.co.uk (engine tuning)
www.turbotechnics.com

Replacement parts:

VAG Parts Ltd
Pembroke Centre
Cheney Manor Estate
Swindon
Wiltshire SN2 2PQ
Tel: 01793 487700 • Fax: 01793 487701

Fontain Motors Ltd
26 Langley Park Road
Iver
Buckinghamshire SL0 9QR
Tel: 01753 650909

Engine and Tuning:

AmD Technik
Unit D2 Telford Road
Bicester
Oxfordshire OX26 4LD
Tel: 01869 323205 • Fax: 01869 323206 • e-mail: info@amdtechnik.com

Ansa Exhausts
Tel: 01978 664468

BurtonPower
617–631 Eastern Avenue
Ilford IG2 6PN
Tel: 020 8554 2281 • Fax: 020 8554 4828 • www.burtonpower.com

G.T. Tuning Ltd
Unit 10, Uplands Industrial Park
Blandford Heights
Blandford
Dorset DT11 7UZ
Tel: 01258 455545/456555 • Fax: 01258 456555

Hyperformance Direct
Tel:01354 741181
www.hyperformancedirect.co.uk

Powertech Filters
Tel: 08450 603020 – for nearest dealer • Fax: 08000 717080
www.powertech.uk.net

Powerflow Exhausts
www.powerflow.uk.com – for nearest dealer

Roadrunner – performance exhaust specialist
379 Nuthall Road
Aspley
Nottingham NG8 5BU
Tel: 0115 978 1173 • Fax: 0115 942 3054
www.roadrunnermotorsport.co.uk

Brakes and Suspension:

Black Diamond – performance braking
Tel: 01254 584784 • www.blackdiamondperformance.com

EVO performance and styling
Tones Garage,
Shotton Road
Peterlee
Co. Durham SR8 4QT
Tel:0191 518 4444 • www.evoperformance.co.uk

Revolution
Tel: 0191 477 0785   www.revolution.eu.com

Urban Racing
Unit 17, Willow Court
West Quay Road
Warrington
Cheshire WA2 8UF
Tel: 01925 444345 • Fax: 01925 231222 • www.urban-racing.com

Styling:

Autoconcepts
Tel: 01202 868833   www.auto-concepts.co.uk

Carisma
Tel: 01905 755558 • Fax: 01905 756269 • www.carismastyle.co.uk

Furious Style
Tel: 01924 455227 • www.furiousstyle.com

Rage Products
www.rageproducts.com

Wheels and Tyres:

Avon tyres
Tel: 01225 707050 – for information and nearest dealer
www.avontyres.com

BK Racing
Deedtrade House
Grace Road Central
Marsh Barton
Exeter
Devon EX2 8QA
Tel: 01392 203044 • www.bkracing.co.uk

Demon Tweaks
0845 330 6252 – wheels tyres and exhaust
0845 330 4724 – all products

Motor-World
Tel: 01274 805350 • www.motor-world.co.uk

Rimstock
Tel: 0121 525 6500 • www.rimstock.com

Smart Car
59 Station Road
Beeston
Nottingham NG9 2AP
Tel: 0115 922 9944

Wolfrace Wheels
Unit 7
Causeway Industrial Estate
Galiford Road
Maldon
Essex
CM9 4XD
0845 330 9896 • www.wolfrace.co.uk

Further reading:

The Audi Quattro Book
Buying, repairing and tuning
Dave Pollard
Haynes Publishing
ISBN 1 85960 403 X
www.haynes.co.uk

Index